NIGEL SLATER is the author of a collection of best-selling books, including the classics *Real Fast Food* and *Real Cooking*, and the award-winning *The Kitchen Diaries*. He has written a much-loved column for the *Observer* for over a decade. His autobiography, *Toast: The Story of a Boy's Hunger*, won six major awards, including the British Biography of the Year.

From the reviews of *Eating for England*:

'A gallimaufry of jottings, including a hymn to gravy, a tribute to dripping and an apologia for mashed swede. Add a sticky mass of sweets and a tart dash of digs at poseurs and food fads and you get a joyously tongue-in-cheek mix'   *Sunday Telegraph*

'Like Slater's joyous descriptions of toast, this book is warm, buttery and just a bit crusty. But his love for these disregarded foods transforms them from throw-away childhood confections into family retainers'
Financial Times

'Slater reflects with equal parts fondness, amusement and distaste on the British way with food, from faggots and gravy through fruit gums ~~and~~ ~~~~'s vinegar to traditional pudd~~~~ *t on Sunday*

'The quirkiest food book of the year . . . 200 essayettes by our culinary national treasure ranging from an in depth consideration of gravy to a dismissal of the jammy dodger'   *Independent*

'Nigel Slater understands as well as anybody how to turn ingredients into a meal, but his big thing is his grasp of how a meal can turn into a new confection in the mind. For Slater, a meal isn't just nourishment, it's memory, nostalgia, excitements and heartache . . . A wonderfully comforting book'

WILLIAM LEITH, *Evening Standard*

'Slater is one of our most talented cookery writers'
Daily Telegraph

'This is food writing with a masterchef. As ever, Slater is also very funny; why, indeed, do the British puddings syllabub, flummery, blancmange sound like they are being enunciated under water?'   *The Times*

'At last, I have found a little remedy for my food-overdose moments . . . My antidote is Nigel Slater's latest, highly addictive, extremely funny and thought-provoking book on British eating habits. I love it – one of my favourite food books this season and it doesn't even feature a recipe'   *Easy Living*

'From mashed swede, home-made gingerbread, funeral teas and dinner parties to washing up, tipping and Heinz ketchup, Nigel Slater celebrates the eccentricity and diversity of the British attitude to food, cooking and eating'   *Woman and Home*

Also by Nigel Slater

Eating for England
Nigel Slater

HARPER PERENNIAL
London, New York, Toronto,
Sydney and New Delhi

Harper Perennial
An imprint of HarperCollins*Publishers*
77–85 Fulham Palace Road
Hammersmith
London W6 8JB

www.harperperennial.co.uk
Visit our authors' blog at www.fifthestate.co.uk

This Harper Perennial edition published 2008

1

First published in Great Britain by Fourth Estate in 2007

Copyright © Nigel Slater 2007

Nigel Slater asserts the moral right to be identified as the author of this work

A catalogue record for this book is available from the British Library

ISBN 978-0-00-719947-1

Set by Rowland Phototypesetting Ltd, Bury St Edmunds, Suffolk

Printed and bound in Great Britain by Clays Ltd, St Ives plc

Mixed Sources

Product group from well-managed
forests and other controlled sources
www.fsc.org   Cert no. SW-COC-1806
© 1996 Forest Stewardship Council

FSC

FSC is a non-profit international organisation established to promote the
responsible management of the world's forests. Products carrying the FSC
label are independently certified to assure consumers that they come
from forests that are managed to meet the social, economic and
ecological needs of present and future generations.

Find out more about HarperCollins and the environment at
www.harpercollins.co.uk/green

For D and P and in memory of M

Contents

Preface

New York, late autumn, and I have just taken the short walk from Central Park to Carnegie Hall, where I am being interviewed for a radio show. It's a bright, invigoratingly breezy day and I'm feeling confident. I know what I am to be interviewed about, and am pretty sure of my ground and even remain unfazed when, at the last minute, I find that the interview is going out live. As I say, I know my ground. And then comes the question, the one I wasn't prepared for, the one where I am asked to describe British food to the listeners.

Do I tell them about the meltingly tender lamb from North Ronaldsay, the famous apple hat pudding with its tender suet crust, or the northern teacake known as the fat rascal? Do I have time to enthuse about the joys of medlar jelly, damson gin and the unpasteurised cheeses made down long leafy lanes in Dorset, Devon and Dumfries? Perhaps I should wax eloquent about Wiltshire bacon, sherry trifle, Christmas pudding, or steak-and-kidney pie with its crumbly pastry and dark and savoury filling? Will there be time to get in name-checks for Scottish heather honey, toasted teacakes, gooseberry fool and Caerphilly cheese? And will they let me squeeze in the glory that is a decent haggis, Welsh rarebit or Cornish pasty?

Or do I tell them the truth? That for every Brit eating our legendary roast beef and jam roly poly there are a million more tucking into Thai green curry and pepperoni pizza. That more people probably eat chocolate brownies than apple crumble and custard, and that it is now easier to find decent sushi than really good roast beef. Should I mention too that despite our love of all that is local, fresh, organic and 'real', we also have a list of edible icons more eccentric than anyone could ever imagine?

It is well known that we have been arguing for years whether gravy should be thick or thin, if pickled onions should be part of a ploughman's lunch, or whether or not jelly belongs in a trifle. I wonder what they would also make of the fact that different counties argue about whether the jam or the clotted cream goes onto a scone before the other, or that more of us apparently use gravy browning than wine to capture the heavenly pan juices of our Sunday roast.

British food is, of course, about roast beef and York-shire pudding; it is about dressed crab, and roast chicken with nutmeggy bread sauce. It is about huge flakes of locally caught fish in crisp batter, eaten from the paper with the sea breeze in your hair, oysters from Whitstable as fresh as an icy wave, Eccles cakes with soft, flaky pastry, and the best bacon sandwich in the world. But it is also about Heinz tomato ketchup, brown sauce and Cadbury's Fruit and Nut. The biggest names on the high street are not Betty's tea rooms but Starbucks and Subway. There are more Pizza Expresses than traditional pie and mash cafés, and more McDonald's than fish-and-chip shops. Looking at some people's supermarket trolleys (oh, come on, you know you have), I sometimes wonder how you could define this country's tastes at all. The internet, by the way, gives approximately 375,000 entries for roast beef and Yorkshire pudding, but over five million for that other great British invention, the Mars bar.

The fact of the matter is that our food culture is about both the gentle, buttercup-scented cheese made in a village barn the colour of honey, and the childish delight of unwrapping a foil triangle of Dairylea. It is indeed true that we make the most crumbly and agreeable oatcakes in the world, but it is the mass-produced cream cracker that has become the culinary icon. And despite producing some of the most delectable pork products in the world, we still love tucking into a bacon sandwich from a greasy-spoon café.

We have a greater wealth of good food in this country today than ever before. When I go to the market at the weekend for my cheeses, vegetables and meat, I am spoilt for choice by the food we produce, and often come home with a shopping bag almost too heavy to lift. In that respect I think of myself as being truly attached to the locally-produced, the artisan-crafted and the hand-made. So how come I also regard a plain chocolate digestive biscuit as one of the finest things this country has to offer?

The British have a curiously broad culinary identity. Only the naïve would now try to pin us down as a meat-and-two-veg culture. You could argue that ours is a rich and multiculturally exciting cuisine, reflecting a country of diverse tastes and open minds; but equally, it sometimes looks as if we are in a state of total culinary shambles. If we hold up a pot of tea with scones and jam as a national treasure (and I do), then why is it easier to find an Italian cappuccino and an all-American blueberry muffin on most high streets? And how is it that while the French almost called a national strike over any suggestion of using pasteurised milk in their cheeses, the Spanish all but went to war to protect their fishing, and Italy gave its Parmesan cheese internationally pro-tected status, we British only truly went into meltdown over the repackaging of the KitKat? (And quite rightly, if you ask me.)

What the French or the Italians may get excited about is very, very different from what most of us in these islands are likely to hold dear. We hold a candle for everything from black pudding to the Custard Cream, feel more fondness for Murray Mints than for a decent veal chop, and are rather partial to leaving our most famous food for the tourists while we ourselves tuck into something from another culture.

This book is my portrait of this curious, often contrary culture, from our adoration of the kipper, the pork scratching and the Rowntree's Fruit Gum to our inability to tip properly in restaurants. I feel that while the heroic efforts of our artisan food-makers have been well catalogued (though still far from well enough patronised), all too little attention has been paid to the food that most of us either actually eat, or at least carry a certain lingering affection for. *Eating for England* is simply a personal celebration of the food this nation cherishes, the rituals we observe, the curious and even eccentric thing that is the British and their food.

Nigel Slater
June 2007

In a Stew

The British make an everyday stew with cubes of beef, carrots, parsnips and onions. They pour a jug of water over it, tuck in a bay leaf and leave it in the oven to do its own thing for four hours. What emerges is grey, meltingly tender meat and gently flavoured broth, comforting and unapologetic in its frugality. It tastes of nothing but itself.

There are formal similarities between our national stew and those of Europe and its neighbours. The knee-jerk shopping list of onions and carrots; the introduction of some sort of benevolent liquid; the convenient habit of leaving the simmering ingredients unattended for an hour or more, are common to all. The southern French recipe will be made with beef rump, its obligatory onions softened in the bright, fruity oil of the region, and its seasonings of orange peel, mauve garlic, sun-scarred tomatoes and, possibly, lavender inevitably breathe sunshine into its soul. Further north, as you potter down the Rhône valley during the *vendange* in October, your day might be punctuated by a paper-tablecloth lunch of cubed beef that has simmered since breakfast with shallots, strips of unsmoked bacon, rosemary and mushrooms in an inky violet-red wine.

The Italians, though less likely to use alcohol, will add body to the simplest stew of boneless brisket with the introduction of a whole, cheap tongue and a gelatinous, collagen-rich cotechino sausage. The juices that surround the meat may look more like ours than do the mahogany-hued French or the paprika-stained Spanish versions, but will be silkily limpid in the mouth because of the goodness distilled from both tongue and cotechino. If a British stew is rich at all, it will be because of the early addition of flour to the meat, the thickening qualities of which give the impression of suavity but add nothing in terms of flavour.

And then, just as we Brits abandon our stew to the hungry hordes gathered at the table, the cooks of other nations will add a vital snap of freshness and vigour to lift it from its sleepy brown torpor: the French their persillade of vivid parsley, anchovy and lemon; the Moroccans a slick of tongue-tingling harissa the colour of a rusty bucket; and the Italians a pool of hot, salty salsa verde pungent with basil, mustard and mint. The Catalans, who, as history would have it, are unlikely ever to spend a penny more than necessary, will even so stir in a final topping of garlic, breadcrumbs, almonds and bitter chocolate fit for royalty.

The basics are familiar in every place; it is only the details, or lack of them, that introduce into the British version the unmistakable air of culinary poverty. Their stews are the colour of mud, blood or ochre pigment, and taste of thyme and garlic, orange and almonds, basil and lemon. Ours is the colour of washing-up water and smells of old people.

Harvest Festival

Apart from Midnight Mass on Christmas Eve, and the time the BBC came to film *Songs of Praise*, my family never really went to church. Yet my father and stepmother always attended harvest festival, usually with me struggling behind with a heavy box of beans, a bag of carrots, and once a wooden crate of windfall apples from the garden.

The little stone church that sat at the bottom of the hill, and where my father's funeral would eventually take place, would have marrows of various sizes, bundles of leeks tied with string, and bunches of dahlias the colour of wine gums stacked outside the door. Inside, loaves of bread and the produce of so many local gardens – pots of asters and bunches of chrysanthemums – were propped around the altar and tucked in the deep stone window ledges. The smell, of over-ripe damsons and yellow sun-flowers, of freshly picked runner beans and home-made raspberry jam, was undercut with a sharp beery smell from the newly harvested hop fields (the church was in the middle of the Hereford–Ledbury–Bromyard hop triangle). I remember feeling that there could be nothing more beautiful than an English church decorated for harvest home. I can't help thinking we still do harvest festival well, although it's a pity that pensioners now insist on bringing tins of Heinz beans. A marrow would be much more pleasing, though presumably a bugger for the old dears to fit in their handbags.

I have always wondered why the sight of a place of worship decorated for harvest thanksgiving is so dis-tinctly British, or at least not especially European. I recently clicked that it is the turning colour of the trees in the churchyards, the honey, orange and deep red leaves, that make the festival so much prettier than it is in warmer climates, whose trees are mostly evergreen (save possibly Vermont, though I have never been there). It is the whole picture, of harvested vegetables, bunches of spiky orange and pink dahlias, and the turning trees that make this a picture of Britain to treasure.

It hasn't always been so. The only reason the Church got involved was to bring a little order to the rampant frolicking and drunkenness that traditionally accom-panied the end of the harvest. It may have been a time for the farmers to say thank you to their workers, but

4

it was also a time for those who toiled in the fields to get off their faces, fight and fornicate. Then a bit of decorum was brought into the proceedings in the shape of the church thanksgiving service. There's the bloody Victorians for you.

The Lunchbox

There is a certain grace with which Indian women glide through the rice fields, lunchboxes in hand. It is as if you are witnessing a slow procession at a religious festival, rather than wives bringing lunch to their husbands. Of course a pink or saffron sari floating in the breeze against a lavender sky will always appear more romantic than one of us popping out to British Home Stores for a cheese and pickle.

School tuck boxes aside, the art of the packed lunch has very much fallen by the wayside. The oblong tin, its lid held secure by a rubber band, is a rare sight now, though the treasures it contains are just as fascinating. By rights the home-made sandwiches should be accompanied by a slice of cake and an apple, though things have moved on a bit. If there is a modern designer version, presumably without the rubber band, it may well now be filled with stuffed focaccia and a little pot of blueberries, or maybe a slice of panettone. The utterly essential Tunnock's Caramel Wafer has no doubt been replaced by one of Ms Gillian McKeith's bowel-opening fibre bars. Hardly ideal, I would have thought, when you are walking through the Yorkshire Dales.

Toblerone

I have always found a bar of Toblerone almost as difficult to conquer as the mountain peaks its design so clearly represents. But beyond the familiar rattle of the bar in its triangular box, and the ragged job you inevitably make of unwrapping it from its foil, lies a quietly classic piece of confectionery quite unlike any other.

Whatever way you try to tackle it, a Toblerone is an obstacle course. It can take a few attempts to break a triangle from the nougat-speckled bar without actually hurting your knuckles, and then, when you finally do, you have a piece of pointy chocolate slightly too big for your mouth. You bite with your front teeth and find the chocolate barely gives, so you attempt to snap it with your fingers, and find that doesn't work either. The only thing left is to pop the whole lump in your mouth and suck.

The pointed end hits the roof of your mouth, so you

roll it over with your tongue, only to find that it makes a lump in your cheek. It is as impossible to eat elegantly as a head of sweetcorn. The only answer is to let the nut-freckled chocolate soften slowly in the warmth of your mouth while rolling it over and over on your tongue. The nutty, creamy chocolate suddenly seems worth every bit of discomfort, and you decide to do it all over again with another piece.

We persevere because we think we like it, which of course we do, but there is more to it than that. Toblerone is a natural step between the cheap, fatty bars in purple wrapping and the posh stuff with its crispness and deep flavour further up the chocolate ladder. Any child who chooses the pyramid of mountain peaks over a slab of Dairy Milk is obviously on his or her way to becoming a chocolate connoisseur.

One often wonders just who actually buys this delightful Swiss-tasting confection, as you never, ever see anyone eating it. Toblerone also has the curious honour of being present in every hotel minibar I have ever opened. Even the one in Thailand, where the only other occupant was a Tetra Pak of tepid tamarind juice and a bottle of mosquito repellent. It is in fact the mini-bar bar, and as you sit alone in your hotel room, letting the pointy, uncomfortable lump of confectionery melt slowly on your tongue, your bar of Toblerone may well, albeit briefly, become your best friend.

The Kitchen Fusspot

They are, in the kitchen at least, late developers. Often genteel, effete, with a little too much time on their hands. Meals emerge from their kitchens with a sense of expectation, each ingredient having been painstakingly sourced, every direction in the cookery book followed to the letter, and inevitably late. The meal has something of the theatrical production about it, albeit amateur dramatics, as if it has all been so, so much trouble. Which of course it has. And don't we know it.

The kitchen fusspot prepares dinner – a charming though slightly too creamy soup, meat with a syrupy, over-reduced sauce, a dessert as elaborate as an Ascot hat and probably just as indigestible – while his guests get more and more hungry, not to say a little pissed. The kitchen, once tidy enough to appear in the pages of *World of Interiors*, now resembles a bombsite of stacked roasting tins, sauté pans and sieves.

Fusspot is almost always male. He only cooks once a month, if that, and needs endless encouragement and ego massage. The production starts several days before, with working out what to cook with the aid of a pile of cookery books of the celebrity-chef variety, and a shopping list, often taken to bed. There may be a tasting of the wines to be served, many of which have come from his own cellar. The menu will be changed every day, each dish chosen for its ability to follow its predecessor perfectly, to match the wines, to show the cook at his most competent.

The directions will have been analysed in a way the poor cookery writer never dreamed of, each line dissected and filleted and then given a jolly good roasting. The kitchen fusspot – let's call him, say, Julian – is a follower of orders, and a cookery writer's nightmare. He cooks without any ability other than that of doing what he is told; a cook incapable of using the merest pinch of invention, imagination or intuition. One wonders – briefly – what he would be like in bed.

Perversely, the fusspot likes nothing better than recipes that 'don't quite work'. 'I think it needs something, don't you?' is his knee-jerk response to every recipe he tries. A little more balsamic, a touch of white pepper, a little Béarnaise sauce on the side. The idea that it might be fine as it is is unthinkable.

Black Pudding

Be it in the form of berries, loops or horseshoes, or maybe sliced from one long, charcoal-coloured dong, the black pudding remains adored and loathed in equal measure. As with tripe, gooseberries and junket, there is no middle ground. Modern squeamishness has led to those of us who turn misty-eyed about such treats being thought of as carnivorous beyond redemption, if not long-lost members of the Addams family. True, our holy grail is a sausage made from the blood of an ox, thickened with pig fat, pearl barley, oatmeal and rusk, but no one should let a little thing like blood and guts get in the way of good eating. What makes the black pudding so delectable, so deeply savoury, so toe-curlingly satisfying, is partly down to good taste, and partly to the pleasure of knowing that our respect for an animal's life extends to the point where we refuse to let even its blood go to waste.

Of course, there is black pudding and there is black pudding. At its worst it is dry, sour and solid. At its best, moist, crumbly and herbal, with a perfect balance of sweetness and deep savour (not to mention being grilled to just the right crispness). I would list a good black pudding as one of the dishes I would want at my last supper, but then it would have to be the very best, and that is where one gets into deep, and very hot, water.

Black pudding fanciers are fiercely loyal, ever ready to challenge anyone who dares to suggest that their butcher's pudding is tastier. The national contests to find the best are always controversial, and cause heated debate. There could even, after a celebratory drink or three, be what used to be called fisticuffs. (A drop or two more of spilled blood is neither here nor there when you consider that it can take ninety litres of blood to make a decent batch.)

Those who trawl southern shops looking for a good pud may wonder if this piece of charcuterie, or perhaps one should say porkery, is about to disappear from the planet, but northerners, particularly those living around Bury in Lancashire, know better. Despite the occasional closure of an outlet here and there, the blood pudding is showing signs of a renaissance, partly due to its being the current darling of many top chefs, who make the most of its savoury qualities as a garnish for other porky or even piscine delights. Black pudding and scallops is much, much more interesting than one might imagine, and is no more strange than bacon with scallops, better known as angels on horseback.

While the notion of a butcher's kitchen awash with blood and rusk may appeal to the more deeply carnivorous, it should be noted that a certain number of sausages are actually made with dried blood, and this certainly seems to pacify the health inspectors. Whether such practices have an effect on the finished article remains a subject for debate. It should go without saying that most recipes remain a closely guarded secret, especially in the crucial and delicate matter of seasoning. And while thyme, marjoram and winter savory are often mentioned, the actual mix of herbs is something most pudding-makers would fight tooth and nail, and no doubt blood and fat, to keep in the family.

I suspect that those who have tried and disliked Britain's proud answer to France's celebrated boudin noir may not have eaten one of the first order. To do so is to experience a piece of craftsmanship that extends beyond sheer cookery. A good black pudding is nothing short of a work of art.

Cake Forks and Sticky Fingers

The Continental cake is slim, shallow, understated. It may be flavoured with almond, pistachio, bitter-orange or rose, and its sugared-almond-coloured box will be tied with a loop of the thinnest pink ribbon, from which it can dangle elegantly from a begloved Parisian hand. English cake is fat, thick and cut in short, stubby wedges; there will be sticky cherries, swirls of buttercream, and sometimes royal icing. What it lacks in elegance it makes up for in enthusiasm.

A French madeleine is a petite almond cake delicately ridged like a miniature scallop shell. An English madeleine is a dumpy castle made out of sponge, doused in raspberry jam and sprinkled with desiccated coconut. It then gets a cherry on top, and if it's really lucky, wings of livid green angelica. It's a case of Proust versus Billy Bunter.

British cakes have a certain wobbly charm to them, and what might be missing in terms of finesse is there in lick-your-fingers stickiness. Fruit-laden Genoa, chunky marmalade, Irish seed cake and glorious coffee and walnut are not delicacies you eat politely with a cake fork, they are something you tuck into with the enthusiasm of a labrador at a water bowl.

Shopping on the Internet – Couch Potatoes

You wander down the virtual aisles plucking your supper off the virtual shelves and dropping it into your virtual basket. No wonky trolleys, no kids throwing tantrums by the iced low-fat doughnuts, no sleazy music sending subliminal messages to get you to buy two instead of one (not that you even wanted one, anyway), and no one at the checkout fiddling to find the right change (Oh, for God's sake, just hand over a twenty, will you?) Add to that the fact that there is no one to peer disapprovingly at your fun pack of assorted crisps, or to look down their ecologically superior nose at you because you have chosen Persil over Ecover, and you have the perfect shopping environment.

Once you have found in which section the kitchen foil and cling film lives, and worked out which of the seventeen sizes of bin bag is the one that actually fits your bin, and eventually mastered the checkout process, you could, in theory, save hours, giving yourself more time to spend with the family, or finally to take up pilates. Pity you can't put petrol in the car online too.

To every up, however, there must be a down, and internet shopping has more than a few. Your inability to find the right dishwasher tablets; the accidental ordering of the wrong colour loo roll (what exactly DO you do with nine apricot-coloured bog rolls?), and the table-thumping, expletive-ridden stress that you suffer when your perfect shopping trip crashes thirty seconds from the final 'Thank you for shopping with Tesco' are usually enough to get even the most fervent net-head making for the nearest Sainsbury's. Add to this the niggling fact that Big Brother now knows how many bars of milk chocolate you get through in a week, or that you haven't needed to buy condoms for a month, and your twenty-first-century shopping trip begins to look a little less like retail Nirvana.

But it goes deeper than this. The occasional online shopping list won't do that much damage to the continued existence of your local shops, but the regular delivery of all you need and more to your door will indeed have a disastrous effect on your cheery local grocer's till. Eventually he will have to shut up shop and move to a cosy flat by the sea, leaving room for a tacky Southern Fried Chicken takeaway to open in his place.

Frankly, you deserve it, and when you come to sell up yourself, you may find your would-be buyers less than keen to move into an area whose local shopping street is littered with polystyrene cartons and tomato-sauce sachets with the corner bitten off. And where do you run to when you need that emergency loo roll?

The Biscuit Tin

Lift the lid of a biscuit tin and you enter a world of chocolate Bourbons, understated, knobbly Lincolns, crumbly digestives and Jammie Dodgers. A secret place where there are lemon puffs, gingernuts, Jaffa Cakes and, if you are lucky, the occasional chocolate finger. No other country whose grocers' shelves I have encountered offers the punter and his purse such a display of sugar-sprinkled flour and butter, blobs of jam and drizzles of chocolate, crème fillings and white icing. We are the everyday biscuit capital of the world (the Dutch hold sway at the top end of the cookie market). What France is to cheese and Italy is to pasta, Britain is to the biscuit. The tin, with its tight lid and cute pictures, is a playground for those who like their snacks sweet and crisp and reeking of tradition.

But there is more to it than that. While some of our

biscuits, such as the Custard Cream and the Bourbon, have become icons of our time, there are others whose everlasting success must always remain something of a mystery. What sort of person chooses a pale, dry Rich Tea when there are so many other more interesting biscuits to choose from? Why would anyone want to eat a wafer that sticks to their lips like glue, or hurt their tongue on the sharp little point of an iced gem? Does anyone honestly like the pink wafer anyway? And who took the last of the chocolate ones? Welcome to the British biscuit tin.

The Digestive

My father loved a plain digestive, though is it difficult to think of him and the iconic biscuit without conjuring up a picture of him trying to slip an entire, unbroken one into his mouth in one go. I can't remember him ever actually succeeding, and if he did it was probably something he did in secret.

It is funny how, whether you had them in your kitchen or not, the digestive always manages to taste of 'home'. It has a unique ability to take you to a safe place, to somewhere you think you remember fondly, even though you may never have even been there. The smell alone, wheaty and sweet with a hint of the hamster's cage about it, is instantly recognisable as a good place to be.

It has been said that this is one of the great dunking biscuits, but I have to disagree. The digestive is altogether too risky. If ever a biscuit will let you down on the way from mug to mouth it is this one, its open, crumbly nature being just not strong enough to hold a decent amount of liquid before it collapses in your lap. But then, like not using the zebra crossing, some might welcome such risks to inject a bit of danger and excitement into their day.

Bread and Butter Pudding

The French cook with their senses, the Italians with their hearts, the Spanish with their energy and the Germans with their appetite. The British, bless them, cook with their wallets. Our ingenuity in matters frugal knows no bounds. When it comes to scrimping and saving, we are the masters. We have taken the worthy 'waste not, want not' to heights unscaled by the rest of the world's cooks. Bread and butter pudding did not come about because someone had the idea that bread, butter and rich, sweet custard would make a sensuous and tender pudding. Whoever it was thought of the idea to use up a few slices of leftover bread and butter. It's a wonder we can hold a wooden spoon, our fists are so tightly clenched.

But then, who can argue with a pudding so calm and gentle, so quivering and fragile, so light and creamy? Bread and butter with its layers of buttered bread, sugar and egg custard is a hot pudding for which we don't have to resort to making a cake mix and steaming it for hours. It is ingenious, and who cares if it just happens to be seasoned as much with meanness as with nutmeg.

Eating Soldiers

A thin slice of buttered toast to poke into the liquid yolk of your boiled egg; an edible teaspoon; a crisp contrast to the runny yolk and jellied white; a jolly idea to get children to eat up their fat and cholesterol – the soldier must have come from the mind of a genius. So christened because it possesses a straight, upright manner, is crisp and uniform in appearance and will stand to attention even when it is up to its knees in yuk. I have never eaten a boiled egg, but I have had a soldier or two. In domestic science, as food technology lessons were once called, we were taught to serve them with mince.

Lunch on a Bench

In summer I often eat lunch sitting on a bench in Hanover Square. The benches are crowded with office workers, shoppers and, invariably, people in black from the Condé Nast offices that overlook the garden, and one has to hover, eagle-eyed, waiting for a spare seat. Other people's lunches are always more interesting than one's own, and it isn't long before I find myself having a furtive peep at the person's next to me. Somehow it *is* always a furtive peep, never an open stare. One always feels guilty about this, though I'm not entirely sure why. If we were in another country – Italy or Sweden, say – we would be much more open about it, and might even strike up a conversation. But this is England, and therefore a furtive peep is all one allows oneself, or gets.

Combating that Sinking Feeling

While most of the world relishes a cup of tea in the afternoon, and perhaps a biscuit or even a slice of strudel, few have gone to the lengths of the British, who have managed to turn a cup of tea and a sliver of cake into a national trademark. It is tea, rather than lunch or dinner, to which we inevitably take visitors from abroad, as much for the cultural experience as for sustenance. Though when we do, it is only fair to point out to them that this is a rare and special treat, and not, like grabbing a sandwich at lunchtime, a way of life. Afternoon tea is the works: scones, sandwiches, cakes, and of course a pot of tea. A cream tea is the edited version: a plate of scones, tea, and if you are lucky a bowl of strawberries. It is what the Cornish feed to tourists.

It is Anna Russell, seventh Duchess of Bedford and reputedly a bit of a glutton, who is generally credited with introducing afternoon tea early in the nineteenth century. At home in Woburn Abbey, she would get her maid to bring tea to her boudoir in the middle of the afternoon, to combat the 'sinking feeling' she experienced between lunch and dinner. I know it well. As the new meal became something of a habit, she took to inviting friends to join her, and soon afternoon tea became a social event. You can always trust the rich to turn greed into a fashion statement.

The wealthy British have long been fascinated by China and Japan. Making a fuss over serving a pot of tea, to which the inhabitants of both countries knew no bounds, was probably seen as our way of buying into their culture. This is why many of our tea services were decorated with Chinoiserie, and goes some way to explaining the preponderance of the once ubiquitous willow pattern china. The Brits never having quite understood the 'less is more' message, the original elegance and grace of the Oriental tea ceremony became somewhat besmirched by the addition of buns and sandwiches, albeit served in dainty proportions.

It seems that no matter how much we adopt a healthy lifestyle, by which one currently means meals that are lower in fat and carbohydrate and with distinctly fewer calories, we still rarely refuse an offer of afternoon tea. There is no real excuse for it; this is not about filling the tank or regulating our blood sugar level. Tea in this sense is an undeniable luxury, a sybaritic pleasure, an orgy of crumbs and cream. Afternoon tea may be the only meal we take that is purely and utterly for pleasure.

Perhaps this simple fact is what keeps its popularity steady, not just with tourists looking for the English experience, but with ladies who gossip, lovers of a certain age, aunts treating nieces and nephews, and those celebrating a birthday. It is something that exists purely to make us feel good about life. On recently arriving for a meeting to find it had been cancelled, one of my colleagues saved the day by suggesting we all decamp for tea and cakes. Our spirits were lifted in a way no other suggestion could have equalled.

Despite the presence of butter and jam and plates of cream cakes, tea remains a quietly polite meal rather than a greedy and excitable one. It is a treat to share with friends and family, rather than business colleagues. You may do business over a full English breakfast or serve coffee during a power meeting, but it is unlikely that the exciting new business plans you are putting forward to your company will be taken seriously if you have a buttered crumpet in one hand. Especially if that crumpet is dribbling warm butter down your arm.

Anyone who doubts that such decadence has a place in a twenty-first-century world of sushi-to-go and travelling cappuccini should attempt to get a table at Betty's in Harrogate on the turn of four. Or perhaps they might like to step into the Wolseley in London's Piccadilly at about half-past three in the afternoon. The latter will be awash with silver pots of Darjeeling and three-tier cake stands piled with all manner of little tarts and fancies, the vast room a veritable sea of tea strainers. The clatter of cake forks amid the gentle buzz of gossip can be seen as a cry for sanity in a world obsessed by calorie-counting and pilates.

The Coffee Percolator

There is a smell in the hall. Dark notes of burning rubber and something exotic, rich, bitter. I push open the door to the kitchen to see my father concentrating intently on a tall, shiny jug plugged into the electric socket by the Aga, its glass lid covered in dancing beads of condensation. Dad is unusually red in the face, and his tie is crooked. He's looking slightly panic-stricken. The Formica counter is freckled with dark brown grains, and the silver jug thing with the glass lid is starting to make an excited plop-plipping sound. Steam seems to be coming from both the machine and my dad.

'It's the new coffee percolator,' announces my mother, who is standing next to him with the noticeably resigned air of a woman who has seen canoes, fishing rods, chess sets, marmalade pans and flashing pink Christmas-tree lights that never worked and should have gone back given the same brief moment of furious attention. I am not quite sure why my father has invested in this particular contraption, especially as we don't really drink coffee anyway, apart from the occasional cup of Maxwell House which we make half-and-half with hot milk. We are simply not a coffee family, and to be honest I am not sure I know anyone who is. Not even the Griptons, and they have an in-and-out gravel drive.

But a coffee percolator we now have, and we all stand round it, excitedly awaiting the result. My father says something about my mother saying she always wanted a perky copulater, which I don't understand and at which she snaps a disgusted, 'And that's enough of that, thank you!'

'Do you think it's ready yet? It's been a while,' says Mum after a suitable period of awed silence. 'I don't know,' admits my father, who then mutters something about the instruction booklet being in Italian, which is odd, as we can both clearly see the words 'Morphy Richards' on the side of the pot. 'Rome wasn't built in a day. Let's give it a bit longer, eh?'

Mum starts to fold some towels, and is in danger of losing interest. I'm wondering what the coffee will taste like, and whether I'm going to have to finish it if I don't like it. My dad gets out the Midwinter china and opens up a box of coffee crystals and another of 'petticoat tails' shortbread, which he arranges on a plate. He unplugs the pot and pours out the coffee, which instantly hits the bottom of the cup and splashes into the saucer and over the table. 'Take the cup up to the pot, Tony, you're making a right old mess,' says Mum, who is now almost as het-up as Dad. 'I know, I know. The spout's too wide, it all comes out in a rush,' he explains, and then we all go quiet.

'Do you think you put enough coffee in?' queries my mother as she puts her cup down. We all sit there, looking down at our pale, watery drink, thin, brown yet peculiarly burnt-tasting. My dad has turned his back to us and is at the sink, battling with the last of the coffee grounds, desperately trying to get them all off the sides of the sink and to rinse them down the plughole. He carefully dries the pot, the glass lid, the little aluminium filter thing that held the grounds, and puts it all back together, bit by bit. Lips pursed, he shoehorns the shiny jug with the glass lid back into its box, slips the instruction booklet down the side, and folds the lid in at the sides. He takes the box out to the garage and puts it on the top shelf, next to the chess set and the box of pink flashing Christmas-tree lights.

Faggots and Gravy

A well-made faggot is a gorgeous thing, tender as mince, but with a defined shape and delicate spicing. But you need a reliable recipe.

I have minced the requisite dark pig's liver, the pork scraps, the bacon and the pig's heart as instructed. I have stirred in the fresh breadcrumbs, the thyme and the sage, the ground mace and the allspice. I have rolled the mixture into tennis balls and wrapped each in a webbing of lacy caul fat specially ordered from the butcher. Laid in an enamel tin like fat dumplings ('faggot', at least in this instance, means bundle) snuggled up together to await the oven and their puddle of onion gravy, they look as hearty as a supper could ever be. The sort of meal you might want to eat on an oilrig, or after a long trek up Scafell.

But my attempts have never matched those of a good local butcher, being just too butch, with too strong a flavour and excessively liverish. The last were coarse and chewy, and weighed on the stomach like lead. Call me a wimpish urbanite, but home-made faggots are obviously for someone who is more of a man than me.

The ones you buy in a deep foil tray from a Black Country market or a Welsh butcher are probably the best bet. The Welsh version can contain oats or apples. Those big-name brands that are no bigger than a scallop and swimming in sweet, rather commercial-tasting gravy, are quite passable on a winter's night. It is almost unthinkable to eat them with anything other than mashed potato and peas, though being a winter dish tradition may have it that it should be a purée of dried peas, known as pease pudding, rather than fresh.

Pros: The glorious gravy and extreme flavour; the frugality of making entrails into something so delicious; few suppers will ward off the cold like faggots and peas.

Con: You are eating pigs' intestines wrapped up in the lining of their stomachs.

The Naked Cook

He has swapped his subscription to *Playboy* for *Delicious*. He scans the 'Kitchen Notes' pages in the *Guardian* and the *Telegraph* for the latest gadgets and the hippest ingredients. He orders his organic meat on the internet and gets his groceries by timed delivery. New-man-in-the-kitchen is more *au fait* with making fettuccine than with putting up shelves. He is more familiar with saucisson than Swarfega, and the only screwdriver he knows comes in a glass with ice and a little dish of olives on the side.

Stroll around London's Borough Market on a Saturday morning and new-man-in-the-kitchen will be there, picking out a nice sea bass for his supper. Still slightly wary of looking too housewifely, he will go for a big fish, or a piece of meat on the bone, rather than anything ready prepared. It is easier to assert your masculinity when buying a whole octopus than a pack of salmon fillets. Mince is obviously a no-no. Cooking has replaced do-it-yourself as a way to show how much of a man you really are. DIY shops are closing like clam shells in a thunderstorm. Anything involving a knife is fine, though he will probably draw the line at pastry. Kneading bread is now seen as just as much a 'guy thing' as knocking down a wall. And he is likely to make just as much mess.

What men's new-found love of cooking shares with do-it-yourself is that even the most botched attempt will lead to him receiving compliments, having his ego massaged, and being told, repeatedly, how clever he is. As the French say, *plus ça change*.

Murray Mints

There is something about the smooth, almost creamy Murray Mint that seems to soothe one's troubles away. I have first-hand experience of finding myself lost, late, cross and frustrated, and discovering an elderly Murray Mint in my coat pocket. Within seconds of the sweet hitting my tongue, my mood changed to something altogether more 'Zen'. Better still, that calmer mood led to me finding my destination in minutes. I was but a block away. Curiously, the soothing effect of the Murray Mint lasts only for as long as you suck. The second you crunch, the spell is broken and the soothing quality completely disappears. Heaven only knows what Freud would make of that.

The Farmers' Market – An Allotment for Wimps

Home to the locally grown and hand harvested, the farmers' market fills the gap between allotment and super-market. I shop there because I want to meet the people who grow what I eat, to experience the joy of seasonal shopping, to be as close as I can to where my food originates from without actually getting my hands in the soil.

The farmers' market works on several levels. It appeals to my need for those who supply my food to have a face rather than to be part of a vast, invisible food machine; it provides an opportunity to buy produce that was picked hours rather than days or even weeks ago; it supports local workers and encourages me to 'do my bit' to cut down 'food miles'. At last, I can put my pound directly into the weathered hand of the person who planted, watered and then dug up the pink fir-apple potatoes I am about to turn into a salad.

And I suspect that, as I trundle up the hill with my recycled bag of cheap corn on the cob still in its fresh green husks and a swaying bunch of three-foot-high sunflowers, it probably allows me to feel just a wee bit smug about those shoppers with their supermarket packet of identically sized, overpriced, cellophane-wrapped green beans from Mozambique.

There are 350 farmers' markets in Britain at the time of writing, from Aberystwyth to York. Dorset alone has ten, London a measly fourteen. Pushed from pillar to post, they find a temporary home wherever the local council will let them set up shop, in school playgrounds, village squares and, ironically, supermarket car parks. The bustling square with its jam-and-'Jerusalem' stalls and green striped parasols is the twenty-first-century replacement for the local outdoor market. The selfsame market that closed down a decade ago, when it could no longer muster the strength to do battle with the invaders

29

from planet Sainsbury. Coming to town just once a week, this colourful gaggle of brave traders in everything from unpasteurised cream to lavender-coloured aubergines has something of the circus about it. We gather round the stalls in awe, gasping at the beauty of a cloth-wrapped truckle of cheddar or a wicker hamper of downy field mushrooms picked at dawn. The farmers' market has become the modern equivalent of a band of travelling minstrels.

Rhubarb and Custard

Is this the infamous Ibby-Jibby Custard Green Snot Pie (all mixed in with a dead dog's eye) of the delightful children's poem?

If it is true that we eat with our eyes, then it is somewhat curious that rhubarb and custard ever made it into our lexicon of national puddings. Perhaps this is a dessert for our hidden child, the one who likes all things ghoulish, spooky and slightly scary. Nothing curdles quite like warm custard poured into poached rhubarb. If you are really unlucky the custard separates into globular forms like those that rise and fall in a lava lamp.

I seem to remember 'rhubarb-n-custard' was the nickname of a particularly acne-ridden boy at school. Nowadays he would probably be called 'pizza face'.

Blood and pus aside, the idea is gastronomically sound enough. Sweet, smooth custard sauce to soften the astringent blow of the fruit; a yellow blanket to put out the acid fire. This is why it is best not to oversweeten the rhubarb, so you get a pleasing hit of both sharp and smooth in the mouth. Scientifically, sweetening the fruit is less effective, as it is the action of the oxalic acid in the rhubarb that curdles the proteins in the egg custard.

Aficionados will surely agree with me that a love of rhubarb and custard, of slithery pink-and-green stems with wibbly wobbly custard, is purely a matter of allowing flavour and sensuality to get the better of aesthetics. That, and trying to forget the spotty kid at school.

If you take the genre a step further you can whip chilled rhubarb and custard into a bowl of sleepy, lightly beaten cream to make a fruit fool. Even then, it will curdle a little, though the effect of pale pink fruit swirled through custard and cream like a raspberry ripple will take any squeamish eater's mind off it.

Fruit and Nut

There are probably few people over thirty who cannot instantly burst into the theme tune from the Fruit and Nut adverts. Which, for younger readers, is 'Everyone's a Fruit and Nut case', sung to the music of Tchaikovsky's *Nutcracker Suite*. It was probably the first famous piece of classical music to be linked to a product, a habit that is now endemic throughout the advertising industry. It is now almost impossible to hear a well-known symphony without a mental link to some household-name product.

It has to be said that Cadbury's Fruit and Nut is an older-generation confection, and hasn't attracted the younger chocolate-eater. The sole reason is the fact that young people generally hate 'bits', and this bar, with its creamy, almost watery-tasting chocolate, currants, sultanas and shards of nut is as bitty as it gets. It has a place in the hearts of the older chocolate-eater, but almost certainly as much for the adverts, and their delightful silliness, as for the chocolate itself, which, let's face it, is hardly Valrhona Manjari.

The Setting of Jam

To the French, the Italians, the Turkish and all the other great preserve-makers, the perfect jam is all about the flavour, the amount of fruit, and a texture poised somewhere in that heavenly state between syrup and a lightly set jelly. To the Spanish, the Swedish and the Bosnians too, it should have visible fruit suspended in a luscious jelly the colour of a jewel in a royal crown. To the British jam-maker, all that seems to matter is 'the set'.

When you mention, casually and perhaps over coffee, that you made jam last weekend, the question will not be 'Does it taste wonderful?' but 'Did it set?' The British jam-maker is obsessed with getting their jam so stiff you could turn the jar upside down and the contents would stay put. The rest of Europe makes jam that slides sexily off the mound of clotted cream and dribbles down the edge of the scone (an exquisite moment if ever there was one). We make jam that sits prim and straight, like a Victorian child at Sunday school.

Commercially produced British jam is easily spotted because it stays put when the jar is moved from side to side. We make jam a little bit like ourselves. A jam that is a bit uptight and reserved, a preserve that wobbles tautly rather than falls off the spoon with a slow, passionate sigh.

Oxo Cubes

The curious fact about Oxo cubes is that we have probably never really needed them. These little cubes of salt,
beef extract and flavourings were, and I suppose still are,
used to add 'depth' to stews, gravies and pie fillings made
with 'inferior' meat. Two million are sold in Britain each
day. Yet any half-competent cook knows you can make
a blissfully flavoursome stew with a bit of scrag and a
few carrots, without recourse to a cube full of chemicals
and dehydrated cow.

Apart from showing disrespect to the animal that has
died for our Sunday lunch (imagine bits of someone
else being added to your remains after you have been
cremated), the use of a strongly seasoned cube to
'enhance' the gravy successfully manages to sum up all
that is wrong about the British attitude to food. How
could we fail to understand that the juices that drip from
a joint of decent meat as it cooks are in fact its heart
and soul, and are individual to that animal. Why would
anyone need to mask the meat's natural flavour? By
making every roast lunch taste the same, smothering the
life out of the natural pan juices seems like an act of
culinary vandalism, and people did, and still do, just that
on a daily basis.

Yet the Oxo cube has played a very important role in
the British kitchen. It gave us a guaranteed, copious

lubricant for our meat, and in the years after the war, the existence of gravy was something to be celebrated. Gravy carried with it an air of achievement and success, but more importantly, it announced a return to normality after years of rationing. It gave us a taste of home as we felt it should be. The red and white box in the pantry was as much a signature of a happy, well-fed home as the teapot and the cake tin. And in the factory-farming years that followed, when modern breeds and cheap production values meant that meat lost much of its inherent goodness and savour, the Oxo was there as a much-needed culinary sticking plaster.

The cube's success also had much to do with the tactile pleasure of tearing open the red and silver foil and crumbling the compost-brown cube into the meat tin, in the style of the 'perfect, squeaky-clean mum' from the television adverts. Sadly, in my experience adding that diminutive cube to the contents of the roasting tin will be forever linked with well-done meat. I can't imagine anyone who appreciated rare beef chucking a load of glutinous gravy on it. If you buy sound meat in the first place, the brown cube is effectively made not just redundant, but an intrusion.

I once had a friend who ate Oxo cubes like fudge, despite their high levels of salt. I often wonder what her blood pressure is now.

Feeding the Elderly

It is December 2004, and I am sitting in an old people's home just outside Birmingham. I'm holding my aunt's hand. My aunt is ninety-nine, my eldest surviving relative on my father's side of the family, and probably the person I am closest to. The home was chosen not for its convenient location, or even its price, but simply because it was the only one I could find that didn't smell of pee.

A woman moves past us pushing a Zimmer frame. As she gets level with us she starts to fart, a sound that goes on for what seems like eternity as she continues to move along in her bumpy, caterpillar fashion. My aunt, who has much the same schoolboy sense of humour as me, starts to giggle.

'What is it about Zimmer frames that makes people trump?' I ask, having heard her parp her way round the communal lounge on several occasions.

'It's all the pushing,' she says. 'Those things take a lot of pushing.' Her giggle becomes a helpless, spluttering cough. 'They just come out, you can't stop them. You'll be like that one day. And sooner than you think. Anyway, they give us too much cabbage in here. We had it three times last week.'

There is cabbage again today. The food is served with more care and grace than one is led to expect of such establishments, but they can't hide the fact that it is mince and cabbage. Individual likes and dislikes are catered for with a resigned smile, and no one is left without help if they need it (and they had a raffle today), but it is still cabbage. The atmosphere, helped by a team of nurses and social workers who show a distinct fondness for their patients, is lively, and particularly jolly at mealtimes. But it is still cabbage.

A quietly-spoken Irish nurse and I struggle to pull my aunt up to the table, sitting her next to Nellie, a dear old lady in a neat cardigan and tartan skirt who constantly asks questions but is too deaf to hear the answers. I can tell she doesn't like my aunt. No one does here, because she has a habit of throwing out the odd racist remark in front of the nurses, some of whom are Indian or from Ghana. She once asked me in something less than a whisper to pass round a box of Quality Street to everyone 'except the black ones'. 'Don't worry, love,' said a gentle, kindly black nurse, 'we know she doesn't mean it.' Sadly, she did, and both the nurse and I knew it.

Pudding is jam sponge and custard, which seems to take the edge off matters. A sweet busy-bee of a nurse asks me if I would like some. It smells cosy, of warm sponge and vanilla, and I am tempted, but decide I might be stealing someone's second helping, so I make do instead with one of my aunt's barley sugars, which I inspect closely, as she has developed a habit of sucking them and putting them back in the wrappers. No one seems to notice that Nellie, who is absent-mindedly humming to herself, is sitting with one hand in her custard. I am tempted to lift it out myself, but then I'm not sure what I'd do with it afterwards, so I pretend I haven't seen it.

A cup of tea and a biscuit becomes a major happening. My aunt looks forward to her milky tea all afternoon, constantly asking if it is teatime. 'I hope I get the Custard Cream this time. They always serve me last, so I'm left with the pink wafers and the broken digestives.' Broken biscuits are inedible to my aunt. In the 1950s, broken biscuits were what you bought when you couldn't afford whole ones.

Feeding the elderly has none of the charisma of feeding children. There is no Jamie Oliver to improve the daily diet of old people. Fewer photo opportunities, probably. What celebrity chef wants to fill his cookbook with pictures of wrinkly people with no teeth? A child with a blob of custard on her chin looks cute; an old person with a blob of custard on hers simply looks demented.

Before my aunt came into the home, where she now gets three perfectly edible meals a day, she lived on Cup a Soup and cream crackers. Not a piece of fruit or vegetable passed her lips for twenty years or more. She could dance, albeit a slow waltz, till she was ninety-seven, then she started falling over and I had to get her into a care home. She was lying on her back in the hall once for twenty-four hours, like an upturned beetle. 'Put me in a home and I'll come back and haunt you,' she once threatened. Now I see her every time I look in a mirror.

Many of the residents have their food put through the mincer, so the only difference between meals is the smell. It's like baby food without the bright colours. My aunt wears a plastic bib to eat now, though she can still feed herself. It's just that most of it ends up down her, rather than inside her. I'm not sure anyone notices. With what ends up around their mouths, down their cardigans or on the floor, I suspect no one realises that what old people actually die of is malnutrition rather than old age. She says she prefers her Cup a Soup, but they won't let her have it, though I do smuggle in a Marks & Spencer crème caramel whenever I can. 'Oh, and bring me a miniature of Bailey's Irish Cream, will you dear?'

It must be interminably dispiriting to cook in an old people's home, to watch your careful cooking, a neatly peeled vegetable or delicately filleted piece of fish, being pushed through the mincer, but that is the long and short of it. The advert in the *Caterer and Hotelkeeper* will insist that applicants must have passed their catering exams, should have the requisite experience and a love of cooking for other people, but it is unlikely to point out that everything the successful interviewee cooks will end up as a purée. One can only imagine they know that easily-swallowed food goes with the territory. Like having no hair or teeth and filling your pants, eating purées is what you do when you come into this world, and again when you go out of it.

Custard

It is difficult not to think of custard with affection. Though it must be said that to the British it is more likely to be vivid yellow and made with custard powder than the calm and pallid crème anglaise favoured by the French. Now even that shortcut has been superseded by ready-made versions available at the chilled counter, some of which are almost indistinguishable from a hand-made egg custard sauce.

The point of custard, or more correctly custard sauce, is essentially to help a dry pudding – treacle tart or spotted dick, say – down the gullet, but it is also a pudding in itself, especially when it becomes the divine dessert banana custard. (I have always found watching slices of banana sink slowly into a deep Pyrex bowl of custard particularly agreeable.) Made somewhat thicker, it is firm enough to be used as a layer, along with sponge cake, fruit and cream, in a trifle.

Yet nowhere is it as welcome as with a steamed sponge. Ginger, jam or raisin puddings are rarely quite themselves without a steaming moat of custard, although somehow treacle pudding is better with cream. The main reason we turned to custard powder was not because of the cost of eggs, milk and vanilla, but because of the sauce's reputation for curdling. 'Curdle', like 'separate', 'split' and 'collapse', is a word that brings unreasonable fear to the hearts of many British cooks. The truth is that nothing can go wrong if you keep the mixture from getting too hot, and even then a curdled mess can sometimes be rescued with a good stiff beating in a cold bowl with a wire whisk.

A Custard

A single 'a' changes everything. In this case it means nothing more than getting a deep pastry tart filled with a nutmeggy mixture of cream, sugar and eggs rather than the expected jug of creamy yellow sauce, 'I'll have a pot of tea and a custard' being a request for a hot drink and an individual tart rather than a dish of sweet sauce.

I fear for the custard. It is as old-fashioned as a slice of Hovis or a clothes brush. It belongs to a world of fire-tongs, antimacassars and black-and-white television. The appreciation of sinking your teeth into the soft, almost damp pastry of a custard tart and feeling the filling quiver against your lip is not for the young. The true enjoyment of a custard (as opposed to the pleasures of custard) is something that only comes with age, like rheumatism, bus passes and a liking for *Midsomer Murders*. I am probably the only person in England to regularly buy a couple of custards from Marks who is still in possession of his own teeth.

The way you tackle a custard is as much a ritual as the way you eat an 'original' KitKat. First you take the tart from its box, then, with the help of your fingernail, you separate the tart from its foil container. It is essential to get it out whole, without denting the fragile pastry edge. Regulars find that pushing up from the bottom helps. You then set about eating the tart either by picking it up and tucking in, or, more likely, as you are obviously a custard tart sort of person, cutting it neatly into quarters. There is something graceful about this last method. What you do with the foil container is not really a matter for this book, but my guess is that it will be crushed, perhaps fold upon fold with an almost origami-style neatness, until it is ready for the bin.

The Economical Cook

Mrs Penny-Pincher saves butter papers. A little wad of them in the fridge door, kept neatly folded for greasing cake tins before she bakes her weekly Victoria sponge. Anyone with a pair of nostrils knows that butter gets fridgy if you don't use it quickly enough, even when you keep it in one of those annoying little compartments in the fridge door. Heaven knows how old some of Mrs P's butter papers are by the time she gets round to using them. She may be saving a penny or two but seems oblivious to the fact that she is actually greasing her cake tins with rancid butter.

She makes stock with every bone and carcass she is left with; uses every manky vegetable in the rack for soup; keeps used tin foil in a pile by the cooker. At the shops, first port of call is the reduced-to-clear bin. Not out of necessity – Mrs P is hardly on the breadline – but out of the possibility of saving a penny or two on a dented tin or a bashed Swiss roll: 'Well, it will be pretty bashed when I've put it in a trifle.' It makes sense, until you consider that you have to buy custard, cream and a tin of fruit cocktail in order to make the most of your thrifty purchase. Normally not known for taking risks, the economical cook is nevertheless willing to take a punt on the can with no label on it. The chances are it will be baked beans, but what the hell, you never know your luck. It might be tinned peaches.

The Voucher Queen

So, you have spent far longer shopping than you intended, getting rather carried away with the new Gary Rhodes saucepan set, and now you are late to pick up the kids from school, and there's a queue at the checkout. Of course there's a queue at the checkout. There is always a queue at the checkout. You start looking at your watch, and then burning your eyes into the neck of the person in front (always helps), daring them to start chatting with the checkout girl, or having the audacity to have some unpriced item in their basket that needs a price check.

All appears to be going well, and you are just reminding yourself not to be such a pessimist, when your heart sinks. The person in front is paying with vouchers cut from a magazine. In terms of annoyance, this is akin to being behind the woman who ferrets in the furthest reaches of her purse for the correct change – 'No, I've got it, it's in here somewhere, dear' – the man whose charge card is refused, the person who finds a leak in their packet of washing powder and has to wait while a runner goes and gets a replacement. Each voucher has been religiously snipped along the dotted line, and despite the honesty with which such people no doubt spend their carefully collected booty, each has to be matched to the contents of the shopping trolley by the cashier.

Standing behind them in the queue, hopping from one foot to the other, and knowing you were late for the kids last week too, you can't help wondering if they are redeeming the voucher against something they would have bought anyway, or are simply buying something to get money off it. You know very well they really would have preferred the almond fancies, but the voucher was only redeemable against cherry Bakewells. So cherry Bakewells it is.

A Cake Walk through Britain

These islands are rich in local recipes, and you could probably eat a different cake in every town from Land's End to the Hebrides. Cornwall's peel-flecked heavy cake would keep you going until you got to feast on Devon's cream-filled chudleighs, before moving swiftly along through treasures such as Somerset's crumbly catterns, Dorset apple, and the sultana-spiked Norfolk vinegar cake. On the way you could snatch a Banbury cake, a Chorley cake, one of Yorkshire's fat rascals or a nice slice of treacly parkin. You might also like to include Richmond maids of honour, Shrewsbury cakes, orange-scented Norfolk sponges and curranty Pembrokeshire buns.

Then there is Pitcaithly bannock (a sort of almond shortbread studded with chopped peel), Westmorland pepper cake with cloves and black treacle, and something called Patagonian black cake, named for the Welsh families who emigrated to work in the South American gold mines. Richmond, Rippon, Selkirk, Nelson, Grantham and Goosenargh all celebrate their existence with something for tea. This is little Britain in a cake tin.

At four o'clock on a Sunday afternoon, cake in hand, we can toast almost any county, city or fair we choose. We can say thank you for the harvest or well done to the sheep shearers, we can salute a wedding or wave goodbye after a funeral. There are temptations to raise a glass of Madeira to Shrove Tuesday and First Footing, to Twelfth Night and Hogmanay, to mop fairs and matrimony. On a Sunday we can thank the Lord with a slice of bible cake or scripture cake, godcakes (but naturally, no devil's food cake) or church window cake, better known as Battenberg. Then there's sad cake, soul cake, sly cake and shy cake; cakes for spinsters, cakes for the navy, cakes for the Queen. There is almost nothing in this country for which a cake hasn't been named.

The Gingerbread Wars

It would be wooden spoons at dawn if any single place tried to claim gingerbread as its own. Instead different territories have laid their claim by adding a little something to the basic butter, sugar and treacle mix. Whether it's beer and ground almonds in the recipe from Fochabers, the oatmeal in Orkney's broonie or the honey that Welsh cooks have been known to stir in, every area seems to have left its stamp. Visitors to Nottingham would no doubt have delighted in the scent of cinnamon from the sticky little cakes sold at the Goose Fair, and while Yorkshire cooks threw in caraway seeds and ground coriander, the Lancastrian bakers next door stirred in marmalade and a teaspoon of mixed spice. Irish recipes have included the worthy note of wholemeal flour and the unabashed luxury of preserved ginger, while Scots drizzled black treacle into their parlies, the little ginger drops so beloved of the Scottish Parliament. The most famous of all, from Grasmere, is barely gingerbread as we know it, being a secret recipe more akin to a biscuit, tender and crumbly and without a hint of treacle, yet blessed with the distinctive notes of brown sugar and butter and the essential whiff of the treasured spice.

Shopping for Meat

Sawdust and scrubbed wood, the wince-inducing scent of fresh blood, men in white coats with Brylcreemed hair and hands like sausages – the traditional butcher's shop was where you went for black pudding for breakfast and a nice chop for your tea. You stood in the cool of white tiles and pale oak butchers' blocks bemoaning the heat outside, or the state of the pavements, or the price of electricity. The butcher's was where you came for a piece of beef for Sunday, or just a bone for the dog and a natter.

Those butchers that are left have a queue only on a Saturday now. There is little time for gossip, and gone are the animals hanging from hooks, which together with the telltale drips of blood on the floor reminded us that our chop was once something that walked and blinked and farted. Today meat is presented to look as little like an animal as possible. Perish the thought that anyone could ever link the lamb on their plate to the gambolling jelly-legged teddy bears in a spring meadow. The headless deer hanging up at Borough Market in London comes as a shock nowadays, sending shivers of Bambicide down your back. It's the hacked-off head that does it, the bloody, gaping neck and the fact that the poor animal always seems to be tied to the fence in a leaping position, as if it was butchered while happily leaping a moss-encrusted log. When Jamie or Hugh kills an animal on television now, it creates an outcry, as if pulling the guts from a pig's carcass has nothing to do with the sausage in our sandwich. The death of an animal for food seems all the more barbaric now that we are kept as far away from the act as possible. In the city it is rare even to spot a pheasant for sale with its feathers on.

If you eat meat and have a local butcher, cherish him. Buy your eggs from him, and your bacon, your butter and your chutney. We need to put as much money in his till as we can if he is still to be there in five years' time. Otherwise a decent pork chop will be as rare as hen's teeth.

Toast – The Story of a Nation's Hunger

I've eaten toast everywhere, from Laos to Luton, and I can say without a shadow of hesitation that no one, but no one, makes toast like the British. Just as you will never find a green curry with quite the subtly aromatic undertones it possesses in Thailand anywhere else, or an osso bucco as celestially tender as one from the hands of an Italian cook, nowhere on earth will you ever be given a piece of toast of the quality you can get on this island.

Why is something you cannot readily put your finger on. Toast is our offering to world gastronomy.

The French have more interesting bread than us, the Italians produce sweeter butter, and no one attends to detail in simple matters quite like the Japanese, yet their efforts at a round of buttered toast are nothing to our own toothsome triumphs. Even when it is not at its best, British toast is perfectly acceptable, unlike the white, flabby versions you might encounter in, say, Greece (where the whole point of toast has surely passed them by) or the laughable attempts you get in the US. No, in matters of toast we excel.

I am not sure that anyone can lay claim to the perfect recipe. How we eat our golden round is distinctly personal. Thick or thin, crisp or soft, gold or brown or black or a bit of all three – and then there is the question of crusts and their retention or removal (it's a minefield, I tell you). Having said that, it is generally accepted that when we ask for a round of toast, we do not expect it to be made with brown bread. Like perfect bed linen or underwear, the perfect piece of toast can only ever be white. Brown-bread toast is for middle-aged people who suddenly decide they should look after themselves a bit more. You might as well eat grilled cardboard. It is permissible for making soldiers for dunking into soft-boiled eggs, but that is as far as it goes.

Frogspawn and Nosebleeds

The idea was that you rushed through your main course to get to your 'afters', so a pudding that is horrible makes no sense at all. It follows that a pudding, dessert, sweet – whatever you call it – must be nice. Naturally, that disqualifies anything that is sloppy, slimy, gummy, cummy or lumpy. It should go without saying that a pudding shouldn't make you gag or retch or heave or shudder. So how come we ever got to eat tapioca? Along with those wicked sisters of the school dining room, sago and semolina, it defies the first law of pudding, in that it must be a treat, something you want to eat, and more importantly something you will agree to be good for. Why should anyone want to tidy their room, be nice to their sister, take the dog out, clean out their rabbit's cage or write Auntie a thank-you letter if their reward is a bowl of snot?

No one else is stupid enough to eat it. Not the French, not even the Germans, for God's sake.

Rice pudding, on the other hand, is the quintessential nursery food. It is simply breast milk for adults. Introduced to Britain by Saxon invaders – how sweet of them to bring us such comfort with their rape and pillage – the pottage of broth and cereals was at first savoury, then by the seventeenth century developed into a sweet mixture of grain, milk and spices. That such dairy-based delights as tapioca and sago puddings have survived in an age of double choc-chip ice cream and black cherry cheesecake is surely testament to the seductive, soothing and security-giving qualities of warm milk.

The word soothing has been attached to more luxurious things than milk puddings, among them Brahms's symphonies, cashmere throws and Cadbury's Flakes. But the genre is still regarded as one of the most successful ways to smooth our ruffled feathers and to make us feel safe and loved. It is also probably the cheapest comfort next to sucking our thumbs.

Puddings of grain, milk and sugar that are cooked in the slowest possible way, usually for three hours or so in a cool oven, seem to belong to a different age. A time when speed was of less interest, where the instant hit of a quick-fix blueberry muffin and a skinny latte was but a distant dream. At first they were sweetened with sherry, cinnamon and sugar, or enriched with eggs. In the eighteenth century they were often covered with a pastry crust – nursery food with knobs on.

Unusually, the modern milk pudding is less rich than its forebears, often being made with nothing but rice, milk and sugar. A long curl of lemon rind or a sprinkling of nutmeg is now seen as an unnecessary addition. A vanilla pod is the only extravagance I put in my own milky puddings, split in half so that some of the fine black seeds escape to freckle the sweet, ivory-coloured milk. Vanilla extract is a cheaper option, but is less subtle. My stepmother always added a bay leaf, until she saw one on *Gardener's World* and realised our bay tree was actually an ornamental laurel.

I don't know anyone who still eats those schoolkid's nightmares sago or tapioca, though they must have their fans. They carry the nickname 'frog spawn' appropriately enough. I have always felt that to be named after amphibians' eggs was actually far too polite for the grey slime they served up as tapioca at school, and have always had my own, rather more gritty, term for it.

Stirring Jam into Your Rice Pudding – Or Not

The world remains divided on whether or not to add some sort of preserve to rice pudding at the table. For every person for whom a blob of raspberry jam, or black-currant or black cherry in their pudding is a step closer to heaven (my father stirred marmalade into his), there are a hundred schoolboys shouting 'Nosebleed!' at the very thought. Perhaps they are right to question the sullying of something so pure, so white, so gentle.

The Nut Cutlet

Most vegetarians would now wince at the thought of a mixture of minced nuts and egg formed to resemble a lamb chop, but thirty years ago the nut cutlet (we are talking mostly Brazils here) was the height of veggie chic. If a non-meat-eater accepted an invitation to a dinner party, it was a pound to a penny they would end up with a substitute chop. The sad thing is that for all the cook's craftsmanship and artistry, the nut cutlet was about as welcome on a vegetarian's plate as a burned sausage.

The Brazil nut is about 63 per cent fat, 25 of which is saturated, which makes it the nut with the highest fat content. Your veggie guests may not thank you for that.

Nuts do not take well to seasoning with either herbs or spices, which leaves most recipes wanting.

Nuts burn at the drop of a hat, so most cutlets were served black outside and lethally raw within.

The price of Brazil nuts being what it is, it became not just a pain to cook something different for 'the veggie', but a purse-splitting expense too.

The vast amount of zinc in Brazil nuts means that a vegetarian male could consume a week's worth at one sitting. All fine and dandy if he and his partner are trying to conceive. A bit of a mess if not.

But surely the most crucial point of all is that if someone doesn't want to eat meat, the chances are they don't want their dinner to look like it either. You wouldn't dream of presenting your Jewish guests with fish carefully manufactured to look like a pork chop. So why wave replica meat in front of someone who clearly doesn't want to see it? British culinary eccentricity mixed with a little thoughtlessness.

A Child in the Restaurant – 1964

The first time I was taken to a restaurant I felt as if I was going to the Oscars. Scrubbed until I shone, tie neatly tied, my socks pulled up straight and my hair combed so I looked like a choirboy, I had been warned to be on my best behaviour. This was parent-speak for remembering to say please and thank you just once too many times, to not let my napkin slide onto the floor, to neither wolf nor dawdle with my food, and most of all to sit up straight. It meant not to ask for fizzy pop, or crunch the ice cubes from the water jug between my teeth, and most definitely not to wipe my lips on my sleeve, a current habit that was 'getting on their nerves'.

We had fruit juice to start, that came in a little Duralex tumbler on a side plate (later, when we went a bit upmarket, it came in a wine glass on a doily); then there was roast chicken with stuffing, peas and roast potatoes; followed by a choice from the trolley of trifle, crème caramel or cream puffs made to look like swans. At least, I thought they looked like swans, but maybe that was my imagination running riot. I chose the swans anyway, or rather, Mother chose them for me, and I thought they were the most wonderful thing I had ever eaten. I didn't ask to get down until the very end. We didn't have coffee. We never did.

Toffees

The British love a toffee, though curiously they are eaten almost exclusively by young boys and older men. There seems to be a toffee wilderness in the middle years. Some chew, some suck, while others do a little of both to get the maximum pleasure from their buttery, creamy sweetmeat. I haven't chewed a toffee since I pulled out a filling with a Mackintosh's Toffo when I was eight, and now tend to suck instead, letting them dissolve at their own speed. Of course the Toffo, for all its waxed-paper-wrapped gorgeousness, was very much a common street toffee, and aficionados have a long list of those they consider more worthy of their molars' attentions.

Toffee slabs – Occasionally, you still find slabs of toffee in transparent wrapping, each square of toffee deeply cut but still part of a slab. The upside is the sheer quantity of toffee you get for your money. The downside is the difficulty of separating each little pillow of toffee from its mate.

Treacle dabs – Sometimes you come across a food that is so dated you cannot imagine who still eats it. Treacle dabs, in their brown-and-white waxed-paper livery, are one of those things. The round, dark toffees that seem like something from the 1940s, if not before, get their characteristic flavour from black treacle and condensed milk, and have a loyal, if small, band of followers. Suck one and you seem to go back to a time you only recall from black-and-white newsreels.

Sharp's assorted toffees – Smooth and long-lasting, these cream toffees in their pink, blue and cream waxed papers have much the same effect on our wellbeing as a Murray Mint. This creamy toffee's ability to soothe has no bounds. Part of the pleasure is untwisting the thin paper, and that first feeling of tooth on toffee.

Milk chocolate toffees – For all my love of dark, bittersweet chocolate, I do prefer my toffees coated in milk chocolate. Whether this is a matter of taste or the need for a shot of nostalgia, I can only speculate; or maybe it really is that the condensed milk and brown sugar content in the average toffee somehow goes better with milk chocolate than with plain.

The Midnight Feast

It is just after twelve, and the late-night film has finished.
You could go to bed, but you feel the need to nibble
something before you finally call it a day. Nothing much,
you understand, just something more than a biscuit and
slightly less trouble than a bowl of porridge. A bowl of
cereal seems plain wrong, as you are probably going to
be eating that again in a few hours. An apple seems too
downright healthy. An orange too much trouble and too
refreshing. You want something warming, if not actually
hot.

Your attention turns to the fridge, even though you
know the contenders are unlikely to be any more exciting
than a carton of past-its-sell-by-date milk and the crusty
remains of a tub of hummus.

You open the fridge door, the light streams into the
darkened kitchen, you peer in hopefully. Quite what
you expect to find you don't really know – a nice round
of rare beef, perhaps, or a chicken drumstick? A slice
of apple pie, or a dish of cold curry? Instead you find
only what you could, in a generous moment, call
'possibilities'.

In the light of the fridge, the rest of the world asleep,
the inedible becomes the edible; a thing of beauty, a
mini-feast. Scraps and leftovers that are on their way to
the bin suddenly become more interesting than you had

first thought: a dried-up bit of cheese, a jug of last Sunday's custard, a bottle of chilli sauce. If only there was something to dip into it.

One suspects the midnight fridge raid is not a wholly British phenomenon, yet somehow I just can't see a Parisian desperately scouring the contents of his salad crisper for something, or more importantly *anything*, fit to eat before going to bed. And let's face it, at that time of night, 'anything' is the appropriate word.

For my money, the ultimate late-night feast is cheese on toast, even if it is made with cheese that a mouse would turn its nose up at, and bread that has seen better days. But all too often sloth overcomes hunger, and one ends up nibbling the dry cheese without bothering to slice it, lay it over the bread and stick it under the grill.

This meal may be the smallest of the day, but it is far from the least consequential. One should never under-estimate the importance of the midnight feast. By its nature this micro-meal must not echo the healthy diet we have, or aspire to have, during the day. A midnight feast should include an element of devil-may-care, or as I call it the fuck-it factor, when you just think, what the hell, I know this is the worst thing I can possibly eat before going to bed, but I'm going to eat it anyway. A salad is not, and can never be, a suitable candidate for the midnight feast in the way a slice of cheesecake, a bacon sandwich or a bowl of cold spaghetti ever can.

But then, just as you thought all the eating was over, there is the middle-of-the-night 'I-can't-sleep' feast, which takes the midnight munchies to new heights – or depths, depending on how you feel about stuffing your face while the rest of the world snores. This is the food of desperation, a last, fist-clenching attempt finally to get to sleep. I say desperate, because this is more than just turning the pillow over, dangling one foot out of bed, curling up in the foetus position or counting saddles of roast lamb jumping over a chocolate log. It involves getting up, finding your dressing gown and coming downstairs. It means having to face opening the fridge door, which is in itself an act of immense significance. It means admitting that there is a problem. 'Perhaps if I have something to eat' is the genuine last resort of the insomniac.

But as you tuck into that portion of cold pasta with tomato sauce you found in the little dish, you can rest assured that at least no one can see you. And, as all dieters know, if no one can see you eat it, then it doesn't count.

Jacob's Club

More than Bourbons, chocolate digestives or even Penguins, the Jacob's Club biscuit had a bit of a middle-class ring to it. My Auntie Marjory even used to bring them out on a plate, like precious gold bars. Everyone had their favourite: mint (green-and-white wrapper), plain chocolate (with golf ball motif, which presumably scared away the children looking for a milk chocolate biscuit), dried fruit (purple wrapper) or the smooth and creamy orange. One of the many pleasures associated with the Club biscuit was attempting to slide the outer paper wrapper off the foil-wrapped biscuit without tearing it, then slowly unwrapping the foil and its paper lining to reveal the thick, oblong chocolate biscuit beneath.

The biscuit's USP was its quantity of extraordinarily thick chocolate. The advertising jingle, which I spent far too much of my childhood singing, was a rather jolly chorus of 'If you like . . . a lot . . . of chocolate on your biscuit join our club.' It must be said that, sadly, that is no longer the case. Several years ago a redesign of the Club seemed to result in a distinctly smaller version of the beloved confection. (It could, of course, be my imagination. Having recently visited my childhood home for the first time in forty years, I felt that used to be bigger too.)

Whatever, the Club biscuit was for many the peak of the biscuit mountain, with its layers of thin biscuit, cream filling and, most importantly, thick chocolate. The fruit one, a sort of chocolate Garibaldi, always seemed like Mum's sort of biscuit, while I was only really excited by the orange version, which was rather like eating a Terry's Chocolate Orange and a Rich Tea biscuit at the same time, though obviously a damn sight easier.

One of the most memorable days of my life was the one when I found an orange Club biscuit that must have been involved in a hiccup on the production line. Instead of a crunchy layer of biscuit buried at the heart of my chocolate snack, there was nothing but chocolate all the way through. One giant lump of pure orange-flavoured chocolate. I felt as if I had won on the Premium Bonds.

Rubbernecking – The Lost Art of Celebrity-Spotting

As a nation of restaurant-goers, the English are probably the world's least subtle celebrity-spotters, making a spectacle of ourselves in a way any B-list celebrity would be proud of. Never let it be said that we aren't world champions in the art of rubbernecking. Not content to discreetly check out the room for famous faces, we then go on to gawp at them like overexcited chimps that have spotted an approaching lion.

It is late autumn, and I'm sitting in a restaurant overlooking New York's Central Park. This place is so smart it has a separate trolley just for the petits fours, which include marshmallows in three flavours made by hand as you watch (and, incidentally, cut into cubes by a begloved waitress with silver grape scissors).

To my left is the actor Roger Moore, his handsome face so well nipped and tucked it appears barely to move even when he sneezes. To my right is an A-list actress, looking serene and jaw-droppingly beautiful in an understated kind of way, and dining with a mega rock star who takes more trips to the loos than an incontinent pensioner. At the back of the room is a table that includes half of New York's yuppie literati, drinking mind-blowingly expensive wine as if it were Diet Coke.

No one bats an eyelid at the assembled celebrities. No one glances or peers, ogles or tries to listen in or, heaven forbid, approach. It is as if they are not there.

London, a chilly autumn evening at a favourite eating place of mine, about nine o'clock on a Saturday night. There is a venerable British actor at one table and Daniel Craig at another (Bonds obviously like their grub), a chat-show host, an overtanned television chef and a much-loved sit-com actor and his mum. They are scattered around the room like so much celebrity confetti.

I am short-sighted, and have taken my glasses off so

I can see the person I am eating with. Everything around me is a blur. As I put my glasses back on to talk to the waiter who is now towering over our table, I suddenly notice the sea of rubbernecks around the room. Left and right, people are peering at the assembled celebrities like curiosities in a museum cabinet. Every mouthful is registered and commented upon by the 'ordinary' punters. While everyone else eats steak and chips the famous names who have, perhaps unwisely, come to a West End restaurant on a Saturday night have inadvertently become the dish of the day.

The Wind in Your Face, a Fish in Your Bag

You crunch your way across the pebbles, forcing yourself through the stiff sea breeze that is turning your hair into a haystack. The ozone stings your cheeks, the seagulls circle and swoop above you, the pebbles underfoot get heavier until it feels as if you are wading through treacle. Ahead of you are the beach huts with their blackboards shouting their catch – 'Place', 'Crabs' and 'Mackrell' – and you know that what they lack in spelling they make up for in caught-today freshness.

There may be some slippery lemon sole with its fawny-grey skin, a lobster waving its claws in anger at having been caught, and indeed spotty plaice so fresh it seems to slither around on the counter. If you live near the coast, this is how you will buy a fish for your tea. Slippery, shining, eyes wide in horror at finding itself lifted from the salty depths, fish so newly caught it smells not of itself, but of the ocean spray, the foam that rides on each incoming wave. You choose your supper, or move on across the beach to the next black hut, the one with the crowd around it.

Then you trudge back across the stones to the car, wondering if you have a lemon at home.

Summer Cooking

While the rest of Europe breathes hot summer colours of ripe red peppers, garlic and thyme, deep purple aubergines and grilled lamb over each other, we paint an altogether more delicate picture. One of gentle flavours and pale hues, of poached salmon and watercress, cucumber and mint, strawberries and cherries, gooseberries and broad beans. Our summer cooking has none of the rough edges of that of the rest of Europe or Australia, whose flavours are loud and proud and edged with enough salt to make your lips smart. Ours are like something out of a Merchant Ivory film, with soft, pale textures and flavours to match. Genteel, mild, polite and placid. The food that accompanies an English summer isn't exciting or stimulating, vibrant or vital, just retiring and calm, like a millpond in July. A watercolour compared with the rest of Europe's hot, passionate swirls of gouache.

The Jaffa Cake

The age-old argument as to whether this thin, dry disc of chocolate-covered sponge is a cake or a biscuit is actually a non-starter. Despite the legal decision that it must be a cake (and therefore not subject to VAT), the Jaffa Cake is a cake in the same way that a Pontefract cake or a slab of Kendal mint cake is a cake. In other words, it isn't. The Jaffa Cake is a biscuit, through and through.

For a little disc of dry sponge, a blob of orange jam and a tissue-thin layer of chocolate, the Jaffa Cake has done rather well. John Lennon was a fan – at least until he went out and bought an entire case of them. It has lasted in pretty much the same state since, though like gingernuts, Pizza Express pizzas and Jacob's Club biscuits, I remember them as once being bigger. But in this case, of course I am wrong.

The JC has a touch of genius to it. The marriage of slightly bitter orange jelly and dark chocolate so thin it shatters as soon as you look at it is a winner. It is intriguing how the top biscuit is always found sponge side up. Curious too, how the Jaffa Cake, like the Cadbury's Flake and the Milky Way, always manages to taste both slightly stale and utterly delicious at the same time. Chocolate and orange is a well-known marriage, but the addition of the raft of dry sponge was probably considered a dangerous move by Mr McVitie. The fact is that it works not just well, but brilliantly. It belongs up there with salted caramels and the Tunnock's Teacake as something that shouldn't work, but does. It is rare that you will find anybody who can stop at just one.

The Village Shop – The Font of All Knowledge and Fairy Soap

We have stopped to buy ingredients for a buttercup-meadow picnic lunch at a post office-cum-grocer's shop in a small, absurdly pretty village in Kent. We have already bought out most of the asparagus stock from the local farm shop, and are wishing we had thought to pack a Primus and a pan. I cannot help overhear the neat, buttoned-up woman in front of us.

'Well, there's been a strange car parked in the lane by

the church for the last hour and a half. I wonder whose it is.'

'Yes, I know. Mrs T mentioned it too. Whoever it belongs to, they must be up to no good. If it's still there in half an hour I'll phone the police.'

You either like the insularity of village life or you don't. Lost? Want a pound of decent dry-cured bacon, a single postage stamp, the plumber's phone number, or to know what time Mrs F left Mr G's house last night? Then the village shop is probably the answer to your prayers. Want to keep yourself to yourself, dislike 'life by committee' or simply fancy a choice of more than one type of dishwasher tablet? Then you are better off living somewhere that passes the cappuccino test. In village life the community is all, so fail to say good morning to everyone who passes as you walk the dog and you risk seeing your photofit on *Crimewatch* the following week.

To those who like the security and sense of belonging that is part and parcel of living in a small community, the village shop will become the epicentre of their world. Country life relies on its existence. It is here you will find everything from a packet of cornflour to some juicy black olives. The fresh food is in many cases locally grown. Tomatoes are likely to come from the market gardener down the road, the asparagus from the farm half a mile away, and the bread to be made by an old-fashioned baker in the next village. That is, if you are lucky. If not, you will find just as disappointing a selection of comestibles as in any inner-city corner shop. It will just come with hanging baskets.

It is curious that village shops manage to stock brand names you thought no longer existed. There is something toe-tinglingly comforting about finding a product that you assumed was no longer made, even if it isn't something you would ever actually buy. It reinforces the idea that your village is a place where time is truly standing still. Or of course a place where manufacturers can dump their old stock now that sophisticated townies have moved on to the next thing. Village shops in general may be a bit low on the lemongrass, but there is something charming about finding yourself in the last remaining place on earth where you can lay your hands on Oxydol and lined writing paper.

The tragedy is that we are losing about three hundred village shops a year. Communities are rallying, and rural councils are setting up business plans to help local shopkeepers, but many will see their sad closure as simply part of the changing face of the countryside. To some, the fact that anyone should wish to live with a septic tank and no buses defies belief, but for those for whom a slower pace and no parking fines is desirable, the survival of the village shop is essential. At the current rate, villagers will have to resort to shopping by post, or doing the unthinkable and moving to somewhere where they can no longer leave a spare key under the doormat.

There has been a strange car parked outside my home in London for three weeks. Of course, no one told the police, they simply nicked the wheels off it.

Tripe and Onions

My father loved a plate of tripe and onions. My stepmother claimed it was like dishcloths boiled in milk. Certainly the waffle-texture of the underside of tripe is not unlike some of the open-work towels my mother kept neatly folded under the sink, though her linen smelled somewhat fresher than a boiled cow's stomach. Tripe is usually bought cleaned and blanched, at least in this country, making its intestinal origins less graphically obvious than on the pieces sold in Spanish or French markets. To put it another way, it stinks. Even Hugh Fearnley-Whittingstall, no slouch when it comes to eating the bits that most of us would happily throw away, calls this particular form of offal 'challenging'.

Tripe is revered by many of the older generation, but I honestly can't recall ever seeing anyone under the age of twenty tucking into it. In fact, you can make that forty. The pros are its extreme tenderness and jelly-like texture. The cons are:

It is an animal's stomach.
Unless properly prepared it smells.
It quivers suspiciously on your fork.
It slithers in your mouth.
It tastes of nothing much.
Boiled tripe and onions is not on the list of things
your home should smell of in order to sell it (unlike
baking bread, freshly ground coffee, or Casablanca
lilies).

Once cleaned of the army-uniform-coloured yuk and
blanched in boiling water, the tripe is ready for sale.
Most people wash it again when they get home (and
sometimes again and again), then cut it into thick strips.
They fry it in butter or oil till golden, then add parsley
and lemon juice. Those who prefer to approach their
offal in a more traditional style will stew it in milk with
onions, and eat it from a soup plate like my dad did. If
you like slimy, wibbly things in milk, then this is probably for you. As acquired tastes go, tripe is surely one of
the most difficult of all to acquire, and despite my being
a dedicated offal man, the charms of tripe and onions
have so far eluded me.

I once spent a while talking to a man who had introduced himself as a 'dresser'. I assumed that he worked
behind the scenes in TV and film, and we talked pleas-
antly about the work involved in looking after the clothes
of celebrities and film stars. I asked who were the most

difficult to deal with. 'Oh no,' he said. 'I dress tripe. You know . . . at the market.'

Aga Toast

Possibly the best toast in the world, and, other than to warm your pyjamas and provide a best friend for the dog, the only real reason to purchase this extraordinary form of cooker. Aga toast is as good as toast gets. The rack comes with your new Aga, consisting of two hinged wire paddles between which the bread is held prisoner and placed directly against the hotplate. Its handles allow you to turn the bread as often as you need to achieve a level of perfection hitherto undreamed of.

The Chocolate Digestive

Dark chocolate and sweet, wheaten biscuit is, rather like goat's cheese and beetroot, smoked salmon and cream cheese, or asparagus and hollandaise sauce, something of a marriage made in heaven. Only simpler. The dark, though far from bitter, chocolate works with the soft biscuit in a way that the combination of milk chocolate and biscuit never could, the tongue-numbingly sweet milk chocolate Hob Nob being a case in point.

Coating a sweet biscuit with yet more sugar and fat in the form of milk chocolate produces a confection that can lean towards the sickly. Despite that, the milk chocolate digestive outsells the dark one. There is a school of thought which suggests that the majority are right, and I occasionally agree with it. Though not in the case of milk chocolate digestives versus dark. It would be like suggesting that the best newspapers are those with the largest circulation.

Dark chocolate, on the other hand, takes this plain, gentle, rather old-fashioned wheat biscuit to another level, adding a touch of luxury without any hint of queasiness. I sometimes think that the dark chocolate digestive is probably the best biscuit in the world. Not that I would ever say so – I couldn't bear all those milk chocolate Hob Yobs shouting at me.

The Rich Tea

It is reassuring, in these days of triple choc-chip, caramel-coated super-biscuits, that the plain, singularly dry Rich Tea has survived. I feel the same about the

Marie, the Morning Coffee and the Thin Arrowroot. In their splendid little book *A Nice Cup of Tea and a Sit Down*, Nicey and Wifey – as the authors somewhat quaintly refer to themselves – claim quite rightly that it is the Rich Tea that 'provides the ground floor on which the rest of the biscuit tower block rests'. It is a very good analogy. You feel that this plain and simple biscuit is where all biscuits started from. It is the white loaf of the biscuit world, and as such has a certain purity to it. Yet it is a biscuit, and therefore a luxury, so I get agitated when people put its straightforward character down. Sometimes a plain, understated biscuit is all the luxury you want. Sometimes, it is all you get.

Fudge

Fudge is toffee for romantics. Melting and honeyed, this fragile sweetmeat lacks the hard-man undertones of a block of toffee, carrying instead the ghost of the British countryside. Most famously sold in the very north and the furthest south, fudge goes hand in hand with thatched cottages and purple heather. As you drive around the Scottish Highlands or the Yorkshire Dales, or along the Cornish coast, you can sometimes feel as if you have stepped into fudge world, a place where visitors are bombarded with packets of sweet brown lumps in cellophane tied up with lilac ribbon. Taking home a packet of fudge is the middle-class equivalent of putting a stick or two of Blackpool rock in your suitcase.

There are essentially two types of fudge: an open-textured, sugary version and a dense, smooth type. Fudge-fanciers fall into two camps: upholders of the crystalline or the creamy. Freshly made, either is delicious if it is buttery enough, the only failure usually being if it is stale, which is all too easy to come across. The more crumbly, sugar-textured fudge is the more difficult to make at home. Some feel that it is a failed attempt at the creamy version. Others prefer it that way. My own attempts at this confection always look like sand that has set, which despite its deep, warm, muscovado butteriness in the mouth is a harsh reminder that what we eat with such relish is mostly sugar.

Ribena

The Land Rover picked me up before six, and I squeezed politely between a witchy woman with eyes like jet and a small child with wild hair that smelled of woodsmoke. They took an instant dislike to me. Posh, I suppose. By the time we got to the field, bouncing up the dry, red-soil track lined with dog roses, my bum was numb and my packed lunch was squashed in its bag, the jam from my sandwiches bleeding through the paper in purple streaks.

We picked blackcurrants till lunch, then stopped for what everyone called breakfast, though nobody spoke to me, then went back to the bushes, tugging the fruit and its stalks from the leafy branches. The smell of a blackcurrant, or pruning my own bushes after harvesting, takes me instantly back to those fields. Now all the fruit is picked by machine, and the schoolboys and gypsy pickers are a thing of the past, but it is good to know that I had my hand in a bottle of Ribena at some point in my life. I remember looking proudly at the bottle in the pantry, with its deliciously sticky gold foil, and thinking it might contain a currant or two that I had picked.

Thirteen billion blackcurrants are made into Ribena each year. I'm glad I don't have to count them. The purple drink was what we were given to fend off colds and 'flu. Though if we succumbed to either, we suddenly switched our allegiance to Lucozade. That was before it was discovered that Ribena's sugar content kept dentists in skiing holidays. Its pimply bottles have been packed with lip-dyeing cordial at the same factory in Coleford in the Forest of Dean for seventy years, and it is only the product that has changed, now having less sugar and added vitamin C. Served iced, it is a surprisingly adult drink if you make it strong enough to bring at least a shadow of the fruit's intrinsic sharpness back.

I have only one bad memory of the drink that I loved most in winter, when my father would bring it up to me in bed, steaming in its condensation-dappled glass. The memory is of one of his regular good hidings. Believe me when I tell you that there is no lie quite so obvious as the one where you try to protest that you have washed your face ready for bedtime while you are still sporting an enormous ear-to-ear purple smile of dried Ribena.

Filling Your Bag

There is a bit of a scrum at the salad stall as fifteen *Guardian* readers all try to get at the wild rocket at once. We might have a Zen-like appreciation of a single, perfect organic onion, but it makes us no less capable of elbowing a fellow shopper in the ribs when we have to. This is food after all, and we are happy to fight for it if needs be.

Elsewhere, arms cross at right angles as the members of an unruly mob reach over one another to get to the Egremont Russet, Blenheim Orange or Michaelmas Red apples. So focused is everyone on filling their hamper with something more interesting than the supermarkets'

Golden Delicious, that stretching across the tangle of forearms for a Peasgood Nonesuch could result in serious injury. It crosses your mind that you could actually kill someone with a well-aimed Bramley.

A late-summer market in full flush will have a selection of fruit and vegetable stalls – some organic, some not – a fish van, several farmers selling ready-jointed meat, and a herb stall. There will be specialist growers offering tomatoes of every shape and hue, but usually Campari, Marmande and the weird and stripy Tigerella, the last of which is actually unexciting in the mouth but draws in the curious shopper like the bearded lady at a Victorian freak show. A table displaying goats' cheeses (rolled in ash, fresh herbs or smoked) and tubs of sharp yoghurt is almost a given in any market, as is a stall peddling turkey-sized free-range chickens and eggs of assorted sizes. These are the work of people obsessed with one product and its quality. It is at these stalls that the real 'finds' often lurk, a rare-breed cockerel for the pot, a chalky cheese of unusual piquancy, a dry-cured bacon to die for. It is worth remembering that the people who produce these are often anoraks. The conversation tends to be a little single-track. I only ask a question if I have an hour to spare.

Old English Spangles

Once occupying pride of place in every schoolboy's pocket, the packet of Spangles died a slow death. After its initial demise in the 1980s, the Spangle was exhumed, put in a new suit and sent out into the world to live another day. Sadly, it survived little more than a day, and died once again. The Old English Spangle, with its black-and-white wrapping and smoother taste – a sort of Spangle that had got off with a Murray Mint – was aimed at the older sweet-lover, and is still thought of fondly by a surprisingly large number. The rumours that the yellow one was flavoured with mustard are totally untrue.

Fry's Five Centres

Similar to the gorgeous Fry's Chocolate Cream, but instead of mint each slim segment was filled with a different-flavour fondant. I remember them as strawberry, orange, lime and another two I could never quite work out. The orange one clearly had the most followers, rather like orange Smarties, and remains the only one to have been elevated to having its own show. The remaining Fry's bars, mint, peppermint and orange, are infuriatingly difficult to find. Fry's Mint Chocolate Cream is a hero, a stalwart of the newsagent's display, a plain chocolate bar proudly holding its head up in a world of fatty, milky, sugary stuff.

Making Coffee

No one save the Americans has embraced instant coffee like the British. Yet no one could have dumped it faster either. Few things mark where we stand in society more clearly than our attitude towards instant coffee. For many of us brought up on Gold Blend, Maxwell House or Mellow Bird's, the powdered stuff is now something at the back of the cupboard left over from when we last had the builders in. It is what we make for the window cleaner or the gas man. Though to be honest, my window cleaner wouldn't thank you for anything less than a Brazilian high-roast cappuccino. Our choice of coffee labels us as surely as our choice of newspaper or radio station. Yet it is said that Elizabeth David was rather fond of instant coffee. She took it with milk in a French porcelain mug shaped like a sundae glass. The mugs were eventually auctioned.

The instant stuff is good for cakes and ice creams,

and for flavouring butter icing for coffee and walnut cake. It is ready literally in an instant, and doesn't require anything in the way of machinery or involve any real washing up. The only small blot on the horizon is that it tastes absolutely nothing like the real thing. It is simply a hot drink, about as close to real coffee as Sunny Delight is to the freshly squeezed juice of a Tarocco blood orange.

Of all things 'Continental' – extra virgin olive oil, good bread, fine wine – it is decent coffee that has been the last to be adopted by the British. For a nation of tea-drinkers this is perhaps to be expected, except that we are no longer the cha-slurpers we were.

We now know our skinny latte from our frappacino, our Brazilian from our Colombian, and indeed some of us will know our Brazilian Rodomunho from our Brazilian Toca de Onca. Yet at home it so often all goes to pieces. No matter how authentic our equipment, how carefully we choose our blends, there is still something that sets us apart from our European neighbours. Where is the richly scented, glossy liquor, the deep caramel-coloured crema, the little bite at the back of the throat? Why do our best efforts so often turn out insipid brown water?

The answer is a question of quantity. For the British it has always been about the amount – a pot of tea, a glass of squash, a pint of beer. What really matters is that our beverages, including alcohol, come in large doses. The idea of grinding, brewing and pouring for a mere tablespoon of coffee in a cup the size of a thimble runs against the national grain. Perhaps it's our inbred generosity that prevents us from taking on board the pleasures of the tiny ristretto an Italian will happily stand and consume at the counter on his way to work. More likely it just seems like a lot of trouble for nowt.

Breakfast

The perfect breakfast is probably the one you eat when you are newly in love. That slight euphoria, the buttering of toast, the flutter of love in your stomach, is possibly a breakfast to beat all breakfasts, if not all meals. The new day ahead, the person in front of you and the sharing of an early meal are charged with energy and hope, not to mention all that fluffy stuff that goes hand in hand with going hand in hand.

Our grandmothers were right: breakfast is something we skip at our peril. Missing out on that first meal is a sure way to end up, mid-morning, with low blood sugar, causing us to tuck into anything that comes to hand, which for most of us will be something sweet. The sugar rush will send our blood sugar level into overdrive, and an hour later our energy levels will crash. It's a vicious circle. Better eat our breakfast, then.

The British, Germans, Dutch and Eastern Europeans do breakfast rather well (the French version is all fat and sugar), and anyone who has done battle at a Swedish hotel breakfast buffet and lived to tell the tale knows that much of Europe takes our grandmothers' sage advice. Traditionally there is protein, fat, carbohydrate and a warm, sweet drink. It is a meal that will 'set us up for the day'. Yet having eaten that first meal everywhere from South America to India, I still think that the traditional British breakfast is as fine a way to start the day as anyone can have.

Bacon, sausage, eggs and mushrooms with a round of toast and marmalade and a pot of tea or coffee is what many of us would choose to be our last meal on earth. It is what we eat when we are on holiday, staying in a hotel or on a long and ridiculously early train journey. On a day-to-day basis, as something to eat between getting out of bed and flying out of the door to work, we are unlikely to break our fast in such a way. The Brits have abandoned tradition, with its extraordinary balance of fat, protein and carbs, for something we feel is more healthy, quicker and less hassle. As I spoon the muesli into my mouth, I can't help thinking it's a shame.

The Chocolate Bar – A Curiously British Obsession

It has been said of religion, and of television, but I insist that it is actually milk chocolate that is 'the opium of the masses'. Barely seven per cent of the country attends church, just 10 million people tune in to the box on any one night. Cadbury's shifts two billion pounds of chocolate a year. One wonders if more people stand at the altar of KitKat than attend mass. Could the Mars bar have more followers than Jesus? We are the second largest consumers of chocolate in the world.

'My Name is Carol and I am a Chocoholic'

Those people who describe themselves as 'chocoholics' are usually anything but. No one who has a craving for a bar of Dairy Milk or a packet of Maltesers can accurately call themselves a chocoholic. In milk chocolate the cocoa content is so low as to be barely noticeable, let alone strong enough to become addicted to.

The self-styled chocoholic inevitably turns out to be addicted not to the precious bean itself, but to the fat and sugar that make up a high percentage of each bar of everyday chocolate. Or more precisely, to the feel that fat and sugar creates in the mouth. The way it coats the tongue, the roof of the mouth and the teeth. It is like wrapping your mouth in cashmere, a comfort blanket for the tastebuds. But with its average cocoa butter content being around 17 per cent, if chocolate is a drug, it is hardly Class A material.

Your Life in Your Hands

It is as if every office in the city has emptied at the same time. Elbows like arrows and bling-encrusted handbags come at you from every direction, each one brandished by someone determined to stop you getting to the poached salmon and watercress before they do, or the crayfish and rocket, the prawn and avocado, even the chicken tikka and cucumber. Nothing, not even the thought of inflicting injury on an innocent co-worker, comes between an office employee and their favourite lunchtime sandwich.

For some, the trip to the local Pret a Manger, Marks & Spencer or Boots sandwich counter is quite possibly the most excitement they get all day; more exciting even than the mayhem that ensues when the photocopier breaks down yet again. In the brief period when I worked in an office, I started thinking about which sandwich I might have as early as 10.30 in the morning, when the rest of Europe had stopped for an espresso and a pastry, and continued right to the moment I stood in front of the serried ranks of chilled doorstops, searching in vain for the one I had been thinking about all morning. Where have they put it today? Why do they keep changing them round? They can't have sold all the chicken and avocado already, can they?

But then, life is never simple, and just as you set eyes on your longed-for prawn mayonnaise you find yourself torn between that and the cellophane pack with the little sticker whispering 'new'. Could this be the sandwich of your dreams, the filling that will change your life, the hand-held combination of comfort and excitement that could make eight hours a day in the human equivalent of a battery cage bearable?

The burning question – is it worth swapping your favourite filling for an as-yet-untried one? The answer will depend on whether you are a trend-setter or just a follower. Perhaps you should wait till someone else in the office has tried the newcomer and expressed their opinion before committing yourself. Of course, you could buy it in addition to your initial choice, but that would make a two- or even three-sandwich lunch, an act of unspeakable gluttony.

And is the whole point of pushing and shoving at the counter really about finishing the bread and its juicy cargo, or is it just about that first bite? After the plastic cover has been successfully peeled from the box in one neat piece, the smell of soft, sliced bread and seasoned mayonnaise has wafted meekly up and you finally push your fingers in between plastic and bread, is the truth that once your teeth have sunk into that first prawn between its slices of damp, wheat-flecked bread, the sandwich loses much of its charm? By the time you are into the fourth or fifth bite, why is it that the thing you looked forward to all morning has suddenly become tedious and sodden, while the last mouthful somehow leaves you feeling just that bit queasy?

And why is the lunchtime sandwich always followed by such pangs of guilt and self-loathing? Until tomorrow, that is . . . some time around 10.30.

Chopsticks at Dawn

The sandwich scene is not what it was. No longer does the crayfish with watercress mayonnaise have the City lunch trade eating out of its hand. There is trouble on the horizon, and that trouble is sushi. At first it appeared unnoticed, hidden amongst the chicken Caesar almost as a joke. Proust questionnaires included the line, 'Have you ever bought the sushi in Pret a Manger?' Most people said no, yet one by one, they started to notice the little plastic trays of orange and white rectangles with their intriguing sachets and bottles and wooden sticks. It wasn't long before someone braver than you brought one of the neat little plastic trays back to the office. They ate not with trepidation, but with confidence and a certain sure-handedness. The war had begun.

Soon, new places opened up selling just sushi and sashimi, which for sushi virgins is the fish bit without the rice. They bore logos the colour of boiled sweets, and came in bags as cool as those of any fashion store. The drinks were different too, made from ginger and fresh mint, rosehips and watermelon. Gloopy mayonnaise had been replaced by searing, bright green wasabi and shavings of bright, fresh ginger. Suddenly the sandwich, with its layers of dough and sweet, icky filling was starting to look a little 'yesterday'.

It is partly the neatness that appeals: the perfectly shaped tray, the dinky plastic bottles of salty soy, stamp-sized packets of hot Japanese horseradish and curiously addictive pickled ginger. The colours shout 'health' and 'low fat', and you start to notice that despite feeling satisfied, you are by no means full. The heavy feeling that accompanies a bread-based lunch has been replaced by a feeling of uplift and vigour. The wasabi has cleared your head, the pickle has made your heart beat faster, you feel lighter and fitter. Not to mention a tad more cool than your colleague munching his way through a triple-decker BLT.

It is early days, but Japanese takeaways are opening faster than you can say 'Skinny miso.' The Earl of Sandwich would be proud of his invention, if indeed it was he who first put his snack between two slices of bread, and of the fact that it has lasted for the best part of 250 years. Yet no one who has seen the yellow and green uniform of the Subway sandwich chain can argue that this particular form of lunch is on the slow but sure fall downmarket. The writing may be on the wall for the ham and salad, the cheese and tomato, and even the all-day breakfast sandwich. Some of us have seen the office lunch of the future, and the future looks very, very bright.

Heinz Tomato Ketchup

Paul Griffiths' mum had decided to abandon the usual birthday party of musical bumps and jelly in favour of tea and a trip to the cinema. We could have fish fingers and chips or sausage and chips. Some of the boys had both, but being a well-brought-up and somewhat timid nine-year-old, I felt that might be seen as greed. (It wasn't, it was just boys being boys, but that was a concept I had yet to master.)

The other boys were boisterously waving around a bottle of Heinz tomato ketchup, hitting it hard on the bottom, its open neck pointing alarmingly at the plate then swinging violently to less suitable targets. It was the first time I had eaten anything other than birthday cake in anyone else's home. It was also the first time I had encountered the joy of wielding a tomato ketchup bottle. Heinz, which is, I suppose, what one means when one mentions tomato ketchup, was banned in our house, and waving the bottle around like a loaded cannon looked enormous fun to a nine-year-old.

Like *A Clockwork Orange* or the ruder parts of *Lady Chatterley's Lover*, the first experience of ketchup at Paul's party had a lot to live up to. To be honest, it was a bit of a let-down, being sweeter and rather less spicy than I had expected, but it was still red and thick and came in a bottle you had to thump. What's not to like? But despite there being something slightly tawdry about a cold plate on its way to the washing up smeared with the remains of bacon, egg and tomato ketchup I have always wanted to like it more than I actually do.

Heinz tomato ketchup, surely the most famous commercial product after Coca-Cola, was launched in 1876, a ready-made version of the slow-cooked home-made 'catsup' of the American Deep South. Traditionally, catsup was made by boiling up tomatoes and seasoning them with cayenne, sugar and vinegar, cloves and cinnamon, and carried a certain amount of interest in its piquant flavour and smooth, but not too smooth, texture. It had rough edges that made it sing in the mouth, and a clever balance of sweetness and acidity. Heinz seized the general idea, removed the rough edges and bottled it. They cleverly held on to the slow cooking bit by making sure the commercial sauce was thick enough to emerge only very, very slowly from its bottle.

There are many for whom the presence of the five-sided bottle is as essential to a meal as salt and pepper. Indeed, I once worked with a top chef who splattered it over everything he ate, though admittedly not until his boss and the customers had departed.

Kia Ora

I was a good boy. A polite boy. A gentle boy. A boy whose only claim to naughtiness had been to fart spectacularly once during school prayers. Yet even that had been an accident, taking me as much by surprise as everyone else.

The nearest I ever came to a deliberate act of bad behaviour was during the Saturday-morning matinee. While the other boys boasted over the latest Roy Rogers adventure about having seen their sisters naked, I just sat there making rude noises with my Kia Ora carton and a straw. The only real reason for buying the warm and frankly rather watery juice drink named after a Maori greeting was the opportunity opened up by its empty packaging.

A straw, a schoolboy and an empty carton capable of making parping noises is an accident waiting to happen. If you sucked hard on your straw, thus removing as much air as possible from the wafer-thin plastic carton, it was possible to make the sort of echoing, rasping noise that has most schoolboys collapsing in fits of red-faced giggles. Devoid of its contents, the Kia Ora carton became an impromptu version of the much-adored whoopee cushion.

On one occasion the film was stopped, and the cinema manager came out to warn the audience that the matinee would be cancelled if the Kia Ora chorus didn't stop immediately. Being the undisputed Kia Ora slurping champion, I took the whole thing rather personally, and never went again.

Tipping, as Only the Brits Know How

London, 11 p.m. He scans the bill, checking off each course, each bottle of mineral water, as carefully as if he was doing the annual stocktake. The words 'service included' tucked away at the bottom stick in his throat. Had it said 'not', life would have been so much easier. Anyone can work out 15 per cent, even after two glasses of champagne and a bottle of Pinot Noir. Now he's unsure of whether to tip on top of the service charge or not. He decides to add a bit extra in cash, because he doesn't want to look mean. Everyone tips on top of the service charge, don't they? The problem is not whether to tip, but how much.

If there was no tip included it would be easy to work out, but he has already paid 12½ per cent, so what exactly does he put down on the plate now? If he adds another 3 per cent, it is going to look as if he forgot his change; another 10 per cent and he is going to look like a fool and his money. A fiver? A tenner? Or does he risk leaving nothing? The bill does say service is included, after all. It is a fine line between flashy jerk and tight git.

'How much shall I leave?'

'It's included, isn't it?'

'Well, yes, but I bet they don't get all of it.'

The waiter comes to remove the coffee cups. 'Excuse me, but do you get the service charge, or do they pocket it?'

The words that in his head seemed like those of a nice guy, who cares about the welfare of the person who has looked after him and his date, now hang in the air like a black cloud.

'Yes, we get the service charge, sir.'

He has been the model diner all evening, and now he feels like a sniping, suspicious weevil. He has accused the waiter's bosses of ripping off their staff, and what is more, made the waiter look like a loser for accepting the situation. What had been so sweet, in the space of one short sentence has suddenly turned sour.

He compensates by over-tipping and rushes out of the restaurant, promising himself he will get it right next time.

Paris, Brussels, Rome. 11 p.m. He pulls out her chair, she moves towards the door and he casually takes a note from his wallet and slips it on the table. The waiter clocks it, smiles, nods and picks it up as discreetly as if he were brushing a crumb from his jacket. The note was neither mean nor cringingly excessive. It was not seen by his guest, and was done in a single, effortless move. Deal done.

Jelly Babies

A jelly baby is more than just sugar and glucose syrup, gelatin and citric acid. Many people are attached to these little baby-shaped gums, almost more than to any other sweet. My personal theory is that this is because they are among the few that have a face.

There are levels of jelly baby, just as there are levels of caviar. At the peak of the jelly baby pyramid is the heavily powder-coated Parr's baby. Slim, long and with a distinctly fruity flavour, this is a slightly grown-up version, the Sevruga of the jelly baby world. The best-known, common-or-garden Bassett's baby appears to have gone in for a bit of surgery of late – it seems now to be wearing a hat, and unless my memory is playing tricks on me, has put on a little weight since it was younger. Well, haven't we all?

The first jelly babies were produced by Bassett, the Sheffield confectioners, shortly following the First World War, and were called 'Peace Babies'. Their name changed in 1953. The white powder, which when sucked or licked away will reveal the babies' true colours, is in fact fine cornstarch, and is there to stop the jellies sticking to one another.

Since a makeover in 1989, each of the jelly babies has acquired a name. I list them only because one never knows when one might need such information. It is the sort of thing that might come up at one of *University Challenge*'s lighter moments.

> Bumper – orange
> Bubbles – lemon
> Boofuls – lime
> Bigheart – blackcurrant
> Brilliant – raspberry
> Baby Bonny – strawberry

I have also heard that the white one is called Blanco. Is this book useful, or what?

Bassett is now part of the massive Cadbury conglomerate, and its baby is smaller than the Parr's, and considered a little mass-market by the legions of JB fans. Three million jelly babies are eaten in this country every week.

This Little Piggy

You curse the jolly green signs attached to the school railings pointing yet more people towards the market, your market. Signs that could assist complete strangers getting to the perkiest, the crispest, the juiciest, before you do. The farmers' market is, after all, supposed to be a secret, where People Like Us can top up our weekly shopping basket with hand-tied bunches of squeaky green spinach and baby red chard for the salad bowl. It is where we can flaunt our jute shopping bags without fear of a sneer, where we can shop amongst other people who care about what they eat and are not afraid to show it.

As you turn the corner, your pace quickens. This is where fruit, vegetables and herbs are sold by the people who planted and harvested them, rather than flown halfway around the world to get to their point of sale. They have grown, baked, bred, caught, brewed or pickled the goods themselves. They have fed the chickens, tended the hives and milked the goats, and are now selling the results direct to the public. Such food has a certain integrity to it. We know, or at least we feel we know, the whole story. More than just a feel-good add-on, this intimate knowledge of our food's provenance has become an essential part of enjoying our supper. All we have to do is to get there before some first-timer swipes the choicest lettuce from under our nose.

The Tight-Arse Cook

Distinctly different from the economical cook because of the fact that they shop and cook not with their senses, their appetite or apparently any sense of self-respect in mind, but purely with their purses. 'Comfortable', even well-off (and never more comfortable than when they have just paid less than they might for something), they delight in nothing more than saving a penny or two on food.

The T-As will happily spend a small fortune on a cruise round the Med or the latest video equipment for their home, but when it comes to food they maintain a vice-like grip on the family purse. Mr T-A will walk to two different supermarkets simply to save 10p on a tin of tomatoes. Of course he doesn't need to, and he spends lavishly enough on clothes, cars, holidays and of course his grandchildren; yet he baulks at paying a penny more than he can get away with for what he and his wife eat.

They must surely be the only folk in the world to check out a website that compares the price of potatoes in each of the major stores before they set out on their shopping trip. Mr Tight-Arse Cook knows that the super-size pack of peaches will never ripen properly (what do they do to them?), yet somehow he thinks there is virtue in buying eight unripe ones rather than spending the same on four beautiful ones that will ripen to a luscious and melting treat. This is simply a case of cutting off your nose to spite your tongue.

Washing Up

After a large meal, Christmas dinner or the Sunday roast, my stepmother, stepsister and I would do the washing up, which of course included the drying and putting away too. I preferred the water-based side of things, finding having my hands immersed in clean, soapy bubbles more engaging than rubbing china dry with a tea towel or, worse by far, putting everything away in its right cupboard. There is something particularly exhausting about lifting up a pile of small plates to insert a pile of larger plates underneath them, but that is part of the deal of 'putting away'.

My stepmother hated the washed-up things standing in the drainer, so my stepsister would take the dripping but painstakingly rinsed plates directly from my hand. Not letting the china drain meant that we got through several soggy tea towels per meal. But as my stepmother enjoyed washing and ironing so much, it didn't really matter. Every now and again a plate or a cup would be rejected with obvious relish, the returned object accompanied by a cry of 'Re . . . ject!' followed by an impatient wait with tight lips while I furiously rewashed it. Doing the washing up was less a natural part of mealtimes than a way to underline the family pecking order.

About 35 per cent of British homes have a dishwasher today, and the figure is growing. Yet there are still those who say they prefer washing up by hand. An announcement that 'Having a machine is not the same as when you do it yourself' is perhaps the last, desperate cry of the woman worried her position might be in jeopardy. The idea that she could be replaced by a machine is a threat altogether too real. Losing her husband to another woman would be one thing, but to a machine that did the dishes would be a humiliation altogether too much to bear.

Mashed Swede

To my knowledge, we are the only country in the world that takes delight in eating boiled and crushed swede. Compared to the elegance of a bunch of asparagus in June or a head of late-summer sweetcorn with its shimmering silks, the swede is hardly the most painterly of vegetables. It is heavy too, surely a warning sign for the shopper.

'Watery' is the usual epithet attached to this most bulbous of the root vegetable family; a truism if it has been cooked for too long, or been insufficiently drained. Beaten to a fluff with salted butter and black pepper, the swede, or swede turnip as the Scots helpfully call it, is quite the most silky of accompaniments to anything overtly meaty. In terms of flavour we are talking mild verging on the tasteless, but few vegetables offer quite the same cooling effect in the mouth after a bite of strongly flavoured offal. Not convinced? Try a spoonful with your next supper of stuffed heart.

We eat a lot of this maligned vegetable in our house. So much so that I regard myself as something of an expert on how to get the fluffiest pile of golden mash (drying the drained vegetables out for a minute over heat helps to prevent a watery end). I can't say I have ever actually bought a swede, it is simply that they turn up in the weekly organic vegetable box, and I feel obliged to use everything. Whether I would walk into the green-grocers and ask for one is something that remains to be seen.

Ginger Cake

Few things will beat a home-made ginger cake, carefully matured for a day or two wrapped in tin foil. Yet this cake, a traditional boil-up of black treacle, brown sugar and butter thickened with flour and made to rise with baking powder and eggs, also responds well to the logistics of commerce. All but the cheapest specimens will probably be moist and dark, though not enough for aficionados. Curiously, a shop-bought one makes a wonderfully sticky pudding if you steam it in a covered pan set over a pan of boiling water. It will need cream, or better still the sharp bite of crème fraiche.

Cream Sponge

There is a type of cream sponge, resembling a Victoria sandwich and sold by chain bakers' shops and supermarkets, that has proved perennially popular. My aunt ate a slice every afternoon almost till the day she died, aged one hundred. Several centimetres high, with a thick band of cream and a thinner one of anonymous jam, it is usually smothered deeply in icing sugar. The fact that it is made in a factory, and has probably never seen real butter or a fresh free-range egg, should render it beyond the pale. Strangely, however, this shop-bought confection can be inexplicably delicious, though one suspects rather more for its soft, duvet-like texture and suspiciously white cream than for its flavour.

Eating in the Street – 'I'll Have That with Wings'

The world eats in the street. The Egyptians, the Thais, the Turkish, the Vietnamese eat in the street. The Colombians, the Brazilians, the French and the Indians eat in the street. In most countries, picnicking as you walk is part of life that only the most self-conscious refuse to take part in. Eating your lunch as you go can, in the right hands, look cool, chic even. In some cases it can even appear sexy, and just occasionally, erotic.

Sadly, the Brits and Americans insist on eating in the street too. When we do it, we never look cool or chic, never romantic or soulful, and certainly never erotic. We just look like klutzes.

For every Thai nibbling a miniature skewer of sizzling, charcoal-grilled chicken, or every package of sweet spices wrapped in a betel leaf eaten in Delhi, there is a Brit biting off more than he can chew. A burger, a parcel of fish and chips, a kebab, can in the hands of an

Englishman resemble lunchtime at a gurning contest. We have neither the charm nor the grace to eat outside the way a Vietnamese can eat a hot spring roll dipped in chilli sauce. Compare, if you will, the way a French student teasingly picks at a baguette on her way to school with the way a Brit attacks his kebab on a Friday night out.

In fairness (and when have I ever been anything but?), it is just as much to do with what we eat as how we eat. In Hanoi, vendors set up their battered charcoal braziers at the side of the road. Their stalls offer rice cakes in banana leaves, neat spring rolls filled with beanshoots and cucumber, bowls of noodles, spicy beef on a skewer and sticky rice. Each vendor will have worked the same patch for years; he will know his old customers and welcome new ones. Anything cooked on the grill with its glowing embers will be paper-thin and mouth-poppingly hot. The portions will be small, but their seasoning, clean, spicy and chilli-speckled, will satisfy as much as any gross-out burger in a bun. The patrons will eat with calm, charm and politeness even amidst the great swirling pot of colour and noise that is Hanoi.

Throwing a Coffee Morning

Before coffee mornings became a way to make money for charity they were purely social affairs, held to welcome a new neighbour into the crescent, or to discreetly show off your new three-piece suite. Now no coffee morning is complete without a collection for the NSPCC or a raffle to raise funds for the church roof. Invariably it will be in aid of something middle-class and respectable. No collections for the local heroin addicts, then.

Coffee mornings started in the 1950s. They were easier to organise then, as most women were at home during the day, busy being domestic goddesses. Fifteen to twenty was considered a good number, as it filled the average living room and created a suitable buzz without people getting too squashed.

Coffee would never, could never, be instant, which would have been social suicide, but was made using ground beans in either a plunge-type cafetière or, during the 1960s at least, a coffee percolator. The most sensible set-up would have been a Cona-type jug, but these were rare in domestic situations, and had a habit of producing a weak brew at the best of times. The usual daily brand of coffee, Nescafé or Maxwell House, would be dropped in favour of Jamaican Blue Mountain or Old Vienna, whose tin would be left casually on display for all to inspect. At least one nosey parker being a given at such an event.

There would generally be jugs of cream and brown sugar, or the gravel-sized coffee crystals which have the added curiosity of never truly dissolving, allowing you to stir as you chat, though you always get a bitter-sweet shot of pure sugar waiting for you at the bottom of the cup. It was part of coffee-morning etiquette to keep stirring and stirring your coffee as you talked – the suburban housewife's answer to playing with worry beads.

There was rarely anything much to eat at such an event, but biscuits were *de rigueur*. Dunking was done, but was regarded as slightly *infra dig*. Digestives would be a rare sight, too common one must suppose, but Abbey Crunch was all the rage, as was a tin of Tea Time Assorted and those lemon puffs no one ever really knew the name of. Garibaldis, or squashed-fly biscuits, rarely made an appearance at such an auspicious occasion, but shortbread would be in great supply – not the short, squat fingers of course, but the more delicate triangles known somewhat appropriately as petticoat tails.

Mugs were an absolute no-no. How anyone got more than half a dozen cups together I don't honestly know, but get them together they did. Along with enough teaspoons and paper napkins for the guests' chocolatey fingers.

One forgets how exotic coffee was at one time, and indeed how stimulating its effect. The beverage was originally used in Europe to prolong the time for which one could pray. Now it prolongs the time one can stand and gossip, *sotto voce*, about the person six feet away from you.

Dress, in the early years, was a twinset (probably Jaeger or something from the local department store with its creaky floors and racks of camelhair coats), earrings, silk scarf and a brooch. Nowadays jeans have crept in, no doubt to the delight of those whose eagle eyes will be on the alert for any sign of bodily imperfection. Nothing quite sets out your stall like a pair of skin-tight Levi's.

Today, the coffee morning is assumed to be another way of saying we want your money, albeit for a good cause. There are websites dedicated to helping us organise successful fund-raising elevenses. No more Blue Mountain, though. It is now the Fairtrade packets one leaves lying around, just to make everyone feel even better.

On bended knee, the black slaves of the Ambassador, arrayed in the most gorgeous oriental costumes served the choicest mocha coffee in tiny cups of egg-shell porcelain, hot, strong and fragrant, poured out in saucers of gold and silver, placed on embroidered silk doyleys frindged with gold bullion, to the grand dames who fluttered their fans with many grimaces, bending their piquant faces –

be-rouged, be-powdered and be-patched – over the new and steaming beverage.

Isaac d'Israeli, *Curiosities of Literature* (1817)

No change there, then.

The Cadbury's Flake

'Look, we're not thinking about oral sex, we're just eating a bloody chocolate bar.'

If the pleasure is all in the melt, then Cadbury struck gold when they launched their ultimate designer chocolate – the Flake. Never before had chocolate melted in such sensual fashion. It is, I insist, a beautiful piece of engineering, easy to hold in its cellophane wrapper, the chocolate having a pleasingly ribbed outer texture that interests the tongue, a smooth consistency that soothes and, being made up of layers of paper-thin chocolate, tends to melt immediately it hits the lips, even before it gets to the tongue, thus giving instant gratification.

The sexual element of the Cadbury's Flake is, I'm afraid, undeniable. I am of course willing to accept the idea that most women never think about sex when eating a Flake (I mean, why would they?), but I will tell you this much. I am willing to bet that the person who first came up with the idea of the Flake was a guy. (Imagine, if you will, the inventor bringing out the prototype at a board meeting, unwrapping it, and putting it to his mouth. Nowadays such an idea would never get past first base.)

Oh and by the way, when exactly did you last see a man eating a Cadbury's Flake?

A Teenager at the Table

The shoulders droop, the head hangs sulkily down, eyes glaring intently at an invisible spot on their lap. Their whole body seems to say, 'I'm not eating this.'

The transition has been slow, from wholehearted tucking in, through leaving a little bit of something on the plate, and then to pushing their dinner around their plate to give the appearance of a meal mostly eaten. What the average teenager fails to realise is that any parent can spot a portion of meat and vegetables that has simply been rearranged.

The final, despairing stage is a complete refusal to eat what is in front of them. Although no parent should take this moment personally, the first time still comes like a shot to the heart. Few things hurt quite so much as a meal cooked and rejected.

There is something in the DNA of a teenager that will, without warning, require all food to be hot, salty and crisp. It is a brief period, and will probably disappear as quickly as the one that finds them developing a temporary allergy to taking a shower.

For crisp, we can read deep-fried. There is little chance of getting a teenager to eat anything that doesn't involve deep vats of hot oil in the recipe. Teenagers are by nature driven towards eating anything guaranteed to make their acne even worse. It is all part of showing your parents you are big enough to go out into the world. If something doesn't give you lung cancer, sclerosis of the liver or a face like a pizza, then it is not worth doing.

Scones and the Sultana Problem

Scones remain the single essential item in the important matter of afternoon tea, more so than sandwiches, cake or even buttered crumpets. A short, tender cakelet of flour, butter and milk, solid yet with an almost Edwardian elegance to it, the scone has Scottish origins, though it appears on tea trays the length and breadth of the country.

A scone is more interesting served warm, when it will certainly get more appreciative oohs and aahs, though by no means hot enough to melt the butter. In order to keep its distance from the sticky-bun type of confection, a scone should be between four and six centimetres high, and should break neatly in half without recourse to a knife. Smaller ones are especially charming. Nothing offered on the tea tray should ever be bigger than two bites, the social embarrassment of choking on a piece of patisserie during the announcement of a particularly delicious bit of scandal being an ever-present threat.

The ingredients, butter, flour, milk and the tiniest amount of sugar, are staples that most of us have in the kitchen as a matter of course. A plateful of scones can be baked in fifteen minutes, and they cost less than the jam and butter we heap upon them. It is the niggling problem of baking powder that floors most of us, and must surely be the only reason we don't get a batch together the minute we hear anyone coming up the drive.

Which bright spark came up with the idea of including sultanas in the mix we shall never know. It is the very plainness of a scone that makes it so eminently suited to a life, albeit a short one, covered in butter, jam and clotted cream. Sultanas turn the whole thing into a dog's dinner.

Bourbon Biscuits

My mother loved a Bourbon biscuit. I often wonder, thinking of her sitting at the table in a quiet moment, could this, with its double layer of chocolate biscuit sandwiching a chocolate cream filling, be the perfect dunking biscuit? No matter how long you dip, it stays intact, and never collapses like a Rich Tea or a digestive, despite the ten holes pierced in its rectangular top and bottom. Even when you pause, mid-dunk, while marvelling at a particularly eyebrow-raising piece of gossip, it will hold its shape. Could this be why the Bourbon is just as popular now as it was in my mother's day? Or is it the way you can prise off the top layer and scrape your teeth down the chocolate cream that keeps this biscuit in a position of such esteem? Or could it be its cocoa-dryness on the tongue? Whatever line you take, there is something quite perfect about this resident of the biscuit tin, and something strangely, in this day and age, luxurious too.

Dairylea

Specialist cheese shops have opened throughout the land, market stalls groan with the weight of truckle cheddars, and we now have artisan-made cheeses to rival almost anything the French can throw at us. Yet somewhere, deep down (presumably under the weight of Colston Bassett and Cornish Yarg), lies a tiny soft spot for a triangle of Dairylea. It doesn't taste of cheese – actually it doesn't taste of anything really – and it is the texture of no *fromage* I have ever met, yet there is something alluring about the disc of foil-wrapped triangles of processed cheese in their shallow cardboard box. Strangely, despite living a stone's throw from a world-renowned cheesemonger, it is to Dairylea that I turn in moments of darkness and despair. While others may hit the bottle, for me there is almost bottomless comfort to be had in a round of thick white toast, made with the worst sort of 'plastic' bread, spread thick and deep with undulating waves of Dairylea.

It is odd that something that tastes of so little can be held in such affection by so many, but then, it is probably a mixture of mouth-feel and nostalgia that draws us in, rather than anything to do with flavour. There is little, save maybe a packet of Love Hearts, which will so instantly take you back to being a child. It is this, rather than anything else, that I suspect is the source of the little foil triangle's never-ending appeal.

Custard Creams

Pale, sweet and bland, the Custard Cream couldn't fail to win over the British. With its two intricately patterned biscuits and thin layer of crème filling, the Custard Cream is more than a biscuit, it is a national institution.

Like malt whisky, slippers and gardening, a liking for the Custard Cream seems to come with age. Yes, there is something faintly custardy about it, though one isn't sure whether that comes from the filling, or from the biscuits themselves. Anyway, the flavour isn't really of custard at all, but of vanilla, albeit a chemical substitute for the real thing.

What to many is the finest commercially produced biscuit of all has won the national Biscuit of the Year award no fewer than twelve times, and it rarely goes out of fashion. You eat them like a Bourbon – that is, either as they come in their original sandwich form, or by twisting off the top biscuit and scraping off the cream with your teeth, or by dunking them in your tea (the biscuit, that is, not your teeth). Like similar buttercream-filled biscuits such as the Gypsy Cream and the aforementioned Bourbon, the filling inevitably adheres more tightly to one biscuit than to the other.

The Custard Cream is the perfect *Archers* biscuit (the dark chocolate digestive is another), by which I mean the sort of thing you want in your hand when you are listening to the enduringly wonderful radio series. Though quite what the biscuit itself thinks of the gay wedding, one can only contemplate.

Modern Shopping

We know how the French shop for food, even if we have never set foot on the rue du Seine. The image of Madame setting out with a wicker basket over her arm and moving wistfully around the market stalls may be as outdated as that of a rosy-cheeked British family grouped round a roast rib of beef, but at least it shows a positive shopping identity. The corresponding British picture, of a harassed couple pushing an overloaded supermarket trolley round the aisles with two hyperactive children swinging from it like apes on a tree branch, doesn't give quite the same cultural message.

The oft-heard mantra that we now like to do our shopping all in one place is the sole reason that so many of our towns now lack a decent row of food shops. The old-fashioned street scene, with its family butcher, fishmonger, grocer's and greengrocer's shops that were once the mainstay of the community, is for the most part long gone. The British love affair with the supermarket has killed off all such streets but those in the most affluent parts of the country. For many who live in inner cities, it is the supermarket or nothing. If we like to do our shopping in one weekly swoop, that is sad evidence that buying food is something the majority can never see as anything but a chore. The fact that choosing what we are going to eat can be something to take enormous pleasure in appears to be anathema to many of us. Food shopping now seems to be just about how to buy as much as possible for as little as possible.

This, I suspect, has less to do with a shortage of time than with the fact that what is being bought is so often mundane and uninteresting. It is easier to delight in buying a bunch of white-tipped radishes or a lush, dew-soaked lettuce in a farmers' market than in dropping a packet of extra-value beefburgers into a shopping trolley. It is the difference between feeding your face and feeding your soul.

Increasingly, though, we are seeing signs of a return to the small shopkeeper, the independent provider of cheese or fish or decent-quality meat. Or at any rate, some of us are. At present it is a small but passionate group, but as more and more of us fall out of love with one-stop shopping, good things can only follow. We will pick up that wicker basket yet. Though whether we will do it as gracefully as Madame is another matter.

The Ritual of the KitKat

I have never actually met anyone who doesn't enjoy a KitKat. Although I have come across plenty, including one or two pathetically snooty foodies, who claim not to, I think they are lying. At the right moment, on the right day, a finger of KitKat is almost irresistible.

Yet one wonders whether it is the chocolate and wafer itself, or something else, that is the real attraction. Yes, it's a perfectly nice bar, but I can't help thinking that its chief draw is the memories it evokes of the lost ritual of KitKat-eating: the indescribably enjoyable art that used to be involved in eating a bar of KitKat before some unimaginative clot decided to repackage it.

Slide the bar from its open-sided wrapper without tearing the wrapper.
Do not puncture the gossamer-thin foil.
Gently rub your finger over each finger of chocolate to reveal the word 'KitKat'.

Slide your thumbnail down the first of the valleys in between the chocolate fingers, thus tearing the foil. (It is important to tear the foil in a straight line, and to keep the edges of the tear as smooth as possible.)

Eat finger by finger, breaking off a new one as you go, rather than all at once.

It must be said that there were some who liked to unwrap their KitKat without cutting the foil. Those who did, inevitably also smoothed the foil out afterwards, so that it was completely flat and smooth. They then rolled it up into a tiny ball. Because of its inherent thinness, KitKat foil made a smaller ball than that of any other chocolate bar.

I must admit to another, far less acceptable, KitKat habit, that of putting my ball of silver foil on the edge of the table and flicking it as hard as I could with my finger. I once got one to travel over fifteen feet.

The Slightly Grubby Wholemeal Cook

What exactly is it about wholemeal flour that goes hand in hand with a lack of hygiene? In theory those who are devoted to it have got it right: the Fairtrade coffee, the sprouted seed, the organic swede, the wooden counters, the politically correct washing-up liquid. And yet, there is something a bit, well, grubby about them in the kitchen. Check those cupboards, with their lentils and dried figs, and you will almost certainly find a few wee-vils, especially in the packet of rye flour tucked away at the back.

Eat here and you will eat healthily. Crunchy carrot salad with sesame and pumpkin seeds, organic broccoli and brown rice and a lovely Fairtrade banana cheesecake. The yoghurt will be goat's, the chocolate barely sweet-ened, and the milk soya. There is a well-worn *Cranks Bible* on the kitchen shelf, and a copy of the *Moosewood Cookbook*, splattered with telltale stains from the day they made the vegetarian lasagne. You can't miss the books, they are on the same shelf as the meditation CDs, the fruit teas and the tantric sex manual.

And if you are tempted by all those scented candles to stay the night, I should check your breakfast muesli very, very carefully.

Cyril's Stew

My father's name was Cyril, but everyone knew him as Tony. Once a year he made a turkey stew, which everyone called a fricassee.

There was much mystique about the fricassee. The remains of the turkey from Christmas dinner were stripped from the bones and cut into small chunks, which would later dissolve into threads as the stew cooked, and cooked, and cooked. Each morsel rescued from the carcass was a personal triumph. Dad wouldn't be happy till the resulting white skeleton resembled nothing more than a parched exhibit from the Natural History Museum.

The meat was put into a pot with onions softened in turkey dripping, thinly sliced green and red peppers, which I should add were all the rage in Britain circa 1964, and something from the spice rack which I always took to be paprika. Certainly it gave Dad's stew the colour of a house brick. I remember there was a bay leaf in there too, and an annual joke about making sure not to swallow it.

Sometimes the stew was made on Boxing Day morning, but occasionally, due to long drives to visit relatives one saw only at Christmas and who were happily forgotten for the rest of the year, it could be anything up to four or five days later. By which time even my father was getting tired of the jokes about the corpse in the larder. The one with a tea towel over its head.

Dripping – The Heart and Soul

Home never seemed quite right without a cup of dripping in the fridge; a little pot of savoury goodness to spread on the Sunday chicken or joint of beef before Mum put it in the oven. Our dripping was always kept in the fridge, in a cup with a broken handle (it strikes me that dripping is ALWAYS kept in the cup with the broken handle). This was, of course, long before olive oil made its leap off the medicine shelf and into our kitchen cupboards. As olive oil took hold as our fat of choice, dear old dripping started to look a bit downmarket. By the time the health police had wagged their mean-spirited fingers at it, dripping was lost.

For dripping, read buried treasure. True to its name, this is the stuff that drips out of the roast beef as it cooks, and collects in the roasting tin. In theory it is just fat and meat juices, but I believe it contains the very heart and soul of the roast, the edible spirit of everything that is glorious about a joint of beef and its crisp, golden fat.

Pour the cooking juices from the roasting tin into a

bowl. They will, as they chill, separate into two halves, a top layer of fat with an underlayer of brown juices, truly a little pot of magic. Once it has chilled, break through the creamy white fat that has risen to the surface, and you have a hidden pool of jellied juices that contain all the goodness of the meat.

Smear a spoonful of dripping on your rib of beef, or use it to start roast potatoes, and you are halfway to heaven already. It is also quite agreeable spread thinly on thick, hot toast and sprinkled with fine salt – a sort of wartime bruschetta.

A Taste of the Future

Before the tea bag became ubiquitous, tea-drinkers had the chance to read their fortune by examining the tea leaves left at the bottom of their cup. A single, wandering line of leaves brought the promise of a journey, a bird would suggest good luck, a bell heralded good news and a flag warned of impending danger. The tea-reading tent was a must-have of the British garden fête, even though it was all too often occupied by a rather dotty spinster with a tea towel round her head and every item from her jewellery box on her fingers.

Of course, others take their tasseography or tassology

far more seriously. The ancient method of telling someone's fortune by reading their tea leaves is particularly
prevalent in Scotland, Ireland and Eastern Europe (the
Middle East tends to use coffee grounds). There remains
something intriguing about having someone, preferably
with more than a little gypsy blood in their veins,
examining the remains of your teacup. The only time I
summoned the courage to have it done, tingles ran up
and down my spine as my future was read. The feeling
was both delightful and faintly sinister. And I can honestly say that I have been on the promised journey,
basked in the successful career, and even been reunited
with the missing loved one. Sadly, I am still waiting for
the tall, dark, handsome stranger.

Floral Gums

Internet sites selling old-fashioned sweets, for whose
existence we should thank God, claim that these charming little gums are one of their biggest sellers. No doubt
this is because they are all but impossible to track down
elsewhere. Perfumed sweets are an acquired taste, yet
these diminutive, multicoloured gems remain the most
asked-for confections at a sweet shop I visited this
week. Sadly, the ones I left with tasted little like I

remember them, and rather more like the bottle of scent I once made for my mother using rose petals, sugar and vinegar.

Sherbet Lemons

Despite our collective sweet tooth, Britons have a yearning for sours – jelly beans, acid drops and soor plooms, and in particular sherbet lemons and limes. Mild and crunchy outside, their thin shells give way under the tongue to an ulcer-producing sherbet filling. You know from someone's expression when they have reached the centre of the sweet.

Soor plooms, incidentally, are glowing green balls the size of a marble, made by Gibbs in Scotland and known for the copious amount of saliva they help produce.

Fray Bentos Steak-and-Kidney Pie

Perhaps it is the idea of an entire meat pie hidden in a tin as thin as a Frisbee, the fact that the pastry is always soggy yet somehow curiously delicious, or simply that there is something magical in watching the pie rise in the oven, but whatever it is about this pie named after a village in Uruguay, we still manage to retain a clear memory of it, even though I suspect many of us have never eaten one. I did try one recently, as an experiment really, and found that some things are best left to our rose-tinted memory.

Eating Outdoors

Essex, early July. I live in fear of the barbecue, its small talk and the awkwardness of holding a glass and a plate at the same time, just as others fear being run down by a bus.

Up to now I have sidestepped the indignity of witnessing otherwise intelligent males presiding over a barbecue while wearing unsuitable attire. By which I mean the sort of apron that succeeds only in emphasising their belly and making them look faintly ridiculous. But just as others will absent-mindedly walk out in front of the number 19, I find myself sitting on a low garden wall doing battle with some rice salad and a couple of chicken drumsticks. Of all the cuts of meat to grill, the drumstick is the least successful, the heat never quite penetrating through to the bone, the meat staying pink even though the skin, on this occasion, is expertly cooked to toasted, golden yellow.

I find that, curiously, almost no one really wants to be here, most of them being only too happy to confide to me that they hate the whole idea of barbecues, but that they felt they 'had' to come. All part of the valiant British spirit, I suppose. Only those who are now shouting loudly across the lawn, the women in unsuitable heels and the men in the sort of shorts that only look good on Italians, seem to be having a good time. And only then because they are half pissed. Short of passing kidney stones, I can imagine no feeling more unpleasant than that of having had too much to drink in the blazing sun.

I have long suspected that it is only the British who behave so anti-socially in the sun. Everyone else knows how to eat and drink outdoors. We stand, they sit. We leave empty bottles on the grass, they put them, elegantly upended, in an ice bucket. They smoke, but it is us who leave our cigarette ends on the lawn, or worse, floating in plastic beakers.

Italy, the tail end of July. The terrace burns your bare feet, the air is still and heavy, even the bees have gone indoors. The table, set with a cloth, two jugs of olive branches, thick plates and green glass beakers, remains curiously cool under the fig trees. There will be a salad of mozzarella and tomato with thick green oil and jagged shreds of basil, a piece of grilled chicken studded with rosemary spikes and salty black olives, and peaches to follow. There will be wine, probably rosé, and it will magically stay chilled throughout lunch. The meal will have an ease to it, a certain effortless style. No one will take their shirt off, no one will have wet patches under their armpits, and yes, the guests will smoke, but no one would dream of leaving a fag end in the grass.

Eating Pomegranates with a Pin

My father ate his pomegranates with a pin. I have never seen this happen anywhere else in the world apart from our sombre sitting room with its ticking clock. He would cut the fruit in half around its tummy, sit it on a plate to catch the drips of ruby-coloured juice, then quietly pick at the glistening, jewel-like flesh, wheedling each diminutive seed out with the end of a pin. Watching him put the pin in his mouth always disturbed me. I imagined him pricking his tongue or lips, but he never seemed to.

This was at a time when this ancient-looking fruit with its little crown was considered an oddity in Britain. In our house, a pomegranate in the fruit bowl, like a pineapple or foil-covered mandarins, was a sign that it was Christmas. Long before we were aware of the fruit's detoxifying properties, or its high level of beta-carotene, we knew of its novelty as a talking point, and its ability to underline our middle-class position to any Yuletide house-guest.

An extraordinary fruit, mysterious, magical, and as entrancing as a snake charmer, the pomegranate has managed to stain almost every shirt in my wardrobe, due no doubt to my habit of eating one most winter evenings while watching television. Its sour, acquired taste makes me feel better about the fact that I am sitting and watching *CSI*. Somehow, bare feet and a pomegranate being superior to carpet slippers and a bag of Werther's Originals.

Mint Cracknel

There was a time when heaven was a Mint Cracknel eaten while watching *Grandstand* on a Saturday afternoon. A slim, short-lived bar that smelled stronger than it tasted, and of which I was briefly rather fond. The very milky chocolate surrounded a rectangular piece of mint crisp that shattered in the mouth. Rather like eating chocolate-covered glass splinters, yet curiously appealing.

Winter Food

Once, our seasons were clearly distinct. The temperature, the sky and the state of the land told us exactly what time of year it was. Now, much has changed, and the seasons seem to be almost indistinguishable. As I write, I have just come in from a lunch of Parma ham, mozzarella cheese and a ripe pear eaten in short sleeves at the garden table, the sun streaming down on my back. It is the first week of March, and only two weeks earlier there was frost on the garden hedges.

That said, we still have an appetite for distinctly seasonal eating, and in many ways it is stronger than it has ever been. Never have we made such a fuss about whether something is in season or not. Books about seasonal eating abound. We are good at autumn cooking, the season of inky blue fruit, pies and crumbles, of pork roasts and game stews, of baked squash and warm figs. Just as the cooks whose homes border the Mediterranean have tomato-and-herb-based summer cooking as part of their soul, it is the cold-weather recipes that seem to run in our veins.

The gentle art of gooseberry fool aside, it is winter cooking at which this country's cooks excel. So perfectly tuned are we to the needs of those coming in from the cold that any cookbook more than thirty years old will read like a dictionary of stodge. Steak-and-kidney pudding, mutton pudding, Lancashire hotpot, beef stew and dumplings, boiled beef and carrots, boiled mutton, pan haggerty, Irish stew – all have an unambiguous warmth and solidity to them. Like the soups, pies and roasts beside them, and along with their carbohydrate-based side dishes, they are there not to tease and titillate our palate, not to lift our mood with their freshness and vigour, but to insulate us to our very marrow. And as for dessert: jam roll, apple hat, cabinet pudding, spotted dick, treacle sponge, rice pudding, figgy pudding, Eve's pudding and their friends will fill every remaining crevice with sweet, nannying stodge.

Few of us can imagine how cold life was, and how hard were working conditions, for our ancestors. Only by looking through a list of what they ate can we confirm just how much they must have needed the sort of fodder we now consider to be outdated, unhealthy and unnecessary.

For the cook-chill generation of eaters such recipes are now museum pieces, and if we make them at all it is out of a mixture of nostalgia and a need to remind ourselves of our culinary heritage. As soon as the weather gets cold, round about Bonfire Night, out come the casseroles and heavy cast-iron pans, the recipes for pies and puddings and the steaming piles of starch to go with them. No sort of cooking gets quite the same energy and enthusiasm stirred into it. And despite its tongue-numbing quantities of suet and flour, nothing will get quite so many cheers.

Despite our modern stew of Thai curries, chargrilled meat and groovy salads, of rice noodles and sushi, of wraps, melts and miso broths, there is still something in our gastronomic DNA that makes us hanker after this type of stodge-fest, albeit occasionally. Few of us need such high-carb, high-fat sustenance any more, but try serving it to friends for supper one cold winter's night and see their faces light up like Christmas decorations.

Is there something in our demeanour, our national psyche, which makes heavy, rather bland food sit so comfortably with us? Perhaps it is the food we need to temper our reserve, inferiority complex and simmering frustration. No matter how much our diet moves on to lighter, brighter, cleaner-tasting food, and our national spirit rises to meet it, there is still somewhere deep in our culinary soul that remains forever winter. A place where pastry crusts, dumplings and suet sponges will always reign supreme.

The Jammie Dodger

Along with the Hob Nob, the Jammie Dodger is one of the very few biscuits for which I feel no warmth. The jam is just that bit too chewy (though I like the way it stretches as you break the biscuit down the middle), the biscuit too pale, bland and sweet. It never quite delivers, yet it has managed to hold the affection of generations of schoolboys. Maybe I'm missing something.

Compare the charms of the Jammie Dodger to the flaky, refreshing Lemon Puff, whose buttery wafer sticks ever so slightly to your fingers, the little chocolate finger that snaps so crisply, the cool, foil-wrapped Mint YoYo, the bland yet curiously moreish Nice, and it just doesn't stand up. Just because it wears its sticky little red heart on its sleeve, that doesn't make it one of the great biscuits, even if it is one of the best-known. Pulling apart a Jammie Dodger shouldn't be mentioned in the same breath as the pleasure to be found in breaking off a piece of (squashed fly) Garibaldi, biting the icing nipple off an Iced Gem or brushing your tongue along the pleasing ridges and furrows of a fig roll. It's like one of those slightly tiresome cheeky chappies off the telly who refuse ever to grow up. You know the ones I mean.

Liquorice Sticks

The flat-ended Bassetti liquorice stick is difficult to put your hands on now, but was once a crucial part of any mixed bag of sweets. Considered by some to be not worth eating without a bag of sherbet in which to dip into, the paddle-shaped Bassetti sticks and their accompaniment of pastel-coloured acidic sherbet powder are made for children, yet with what I would have thought were rather adult flavourings of liquorice and sour sherbet. A clear sign that children like stronger tastes than many manufacturers give them credit for.

Liquorice Wood

Real brown liquorice root, this was something for the cool, tough guy who would rather have been seen dead than with a quarter of sherbet lemons. Like a straw, you put it in the corner of your mouth and chewed, and chewed, and chewed, though to do it justice you really needed a cowboy hat too. Rarely seen nowadays.

The Chocolate Finger and That One with the Hole In

In a new tin the chocolate biscuits sit, glossy and unblemished, slotted in towering stacks in their cellophane compartments. The chocolate finger is almost always the first to disappear, but then it is almost irresistible not to stick your finger in the other chocolate one, the one with the hole in, and to lift it from its pile without touching the edges. My guess is that the designer reckoned the temptation of sticking your finger in a hole (like that of sticking your tongue in a Polo Mint) would be enough to secure the biscuit's popularity. Having said that, it is odd that no one actually knows the name of it – it is just known as the one with the hole in it.

There was a time when the biscuits were kept separate from one another by carefully folded corrugated white paper, then came the controversial crunchy red cellophane compartment divider, and then finally a clear plastic one.

Of course, the temptation of scrunching the plastic liner is just too great for most of us, and I am sure I can't be the only person who has ever tipped the last few biscuits into the shiny, naked tin in order to attack the red plastic casing – which explains why the average biscuit tin always, always has a dog-eared Custard Cream and a pink wafer in it. And there they remain, long after new packets of biscuits, none ever quite as exciting as the originals, are unwrapped and sent clattering into the shiny tin.

A Good Roasting

Nothing quite prepares you for the sheer majesty of the English roast. The meltingly tender meat, the crisp-edged fat, the deep savour of the gravy, and indeed for the host of extras that keep the meat company on the plate. Roast lamb alone can have mint sauce, redcurrant jelly, green vegetables and potatoes. Beef often arrives at the table with a coterie of Yorkshire pudding, horse-radish sauce, hot, bright-yellow mustard, roast potatoes and parsnips, plus the usual vegetables. Pork gets apple purée and sage-and-onion stuffing. We are superlative roasters, especially those of us who know when to stop, leaving beef and lamb with a pink centre, and to let it rest a while before we carve so that the fibres take up the juices.

The cuts will vary according to our taste and budget. Fillet is the footballer's wife of the butcher's block, slim, flashy and with debatable taste (and not an inch of fat to be seen). Anything on the bone is likely to be more interesting than lean meat, immediately lending succulence and savour. Pity it makes it such a bugger to carve.

Roast beef dominates the imagination of tourists hunting for the authentic taste of British cooking. They are not alone, the plate of Sunday best being at the top of most people's list of what we do best: the lustworthy pink flesh, the generosity, the lip-smacking crusty bits around the edge. You can almost feel a nation puffing out its collective chest. It is served in layer after layer of finely carved slices, with a jug of gravy made from its juices and savoury detritus stuck to the roasting tin, and ringed with a display of vegetables including cauliflower cheese, roast potatoes, buttered cabbage and carrots to bring colour to its cheeks. A pool of creamed horseradish root, a dab of Norwich's finest yellow stuff, and enough gravy to float a boat. A dog's dinner? Well, yes, but a glorious dinner too, one that allows the nation to think, for one delicious moment, that we have food that is a match for anyone's. A steaming plate of national pride, something we can summon up in any argument about our contribution to The World's Great Dishes.

Boiled Brussels Sprouts

A beautiful, mysterious thing when seen on the stalk in a foggy field in January, the Brussels sprout has a fairytale look to it. One could imagine the splendid stalks towering over small creatures, a forest for them in which to live. A pity then that the vegetable shares so many of its attributes with a fart. The smell of a room in which a pan of sprouts has recently been boiled is downright offensive to anyone other than the cook, much in the way that your own flatulence is acceptable, but not other people's. Very different from the room that delights in a vague whiff of roast potatoes, grilled aubergines or baked tomatoes – these are smells that bring us to the table. Perhaps it should come as no surprise then that the Brussels sprout is a favourite vegetable in a nation with a well-established lavatorial sense of humour. Vegetables can tell us a lot about a country.

The sprout has been with us since the nineteenth century, and with the Belgians since the Middle Ages, when they were known appetisingly as *sproq*. The Belgian habit of serving them up in melted butter is one we have taken to, but is far from the most interesting. Bacon or cream can have a ravishing effect on any brassica, but especially this one.

It is unfortunate that the sprout's flavour is neither as authoritative as the handsome, plume-like leaves of cavolo nero, nor as fresh and gentle as that of spring cabbage. They can take on a bitter edge, too. Those who cut a cross in the base of each one before cooking must either have too much time on their hands or actually like the idea of sodden greens. Jane Grigson gives a recipe for them where they are briefly boiled, then packed into a gratin dish and covered with a sauce made from chicken stock, béchamel, tarragon, cream, cayenne, gruyère, parmesan and breadcrumbs. Delicious, but a cover-up job if ever there was one. A modern version is Rose Prince's way with sprout tops (which for some reason are less sulphurous than the buttons themselves), where she simply flavours simmering cream with rosemary and lemon juice, then tosses the lightly cooked leaves in it.

Brussels are an essential part of the Christmas meal, where they are often served with chestnuts, and which does little for them. They are truly a winter vegetable, sweetening up after a bout of proper cold. Gardeners love them for the ease with which they can be picked from the stem in freezing weather, rather than dug from the frozen ground like so many other winter vegetables. They last better on the stalk than in a paper bag in the fridge, and this has become a new-fangled way to purchase them. Fine, if you don't mind carrying them back from the farmers' market like a particularly knobbly umbrella. There is something rather neat about picking up a green net bag of them from the supermarket, like a bag of edible marbles.

It is not surprising that we have but one way to cook this member of the mustard family. Boiling food is in our blood. But step outside the box and the little green nodules can offer so much more interest: shredded and tossed in hot oil with garlic; chopped and folded into cream flavoured with slow-cooked garlic; stir-fried with ginger and spring onion; shaken in a pan with shards of crisp bacon and breadcrumbs; sliced and sautéed in olive oil then seasoned and tossed with grated parmesan, letting it colour and melt in the oil. The curious thing about these treatments is not so much that they are utterly delicious, but that the finished dish has not even the merest trace of sulphur.

I still think it's pretty odd that people want to eat something that smells the way they do. 'Are we having sprouts for tea, or has somebody let one go?'

Pontefract Cakes

Not in fact a cake, but a flat disc, shiny and black as a top hat, flavoured with liquorice and aniseed. According to Laura Mason and Catherine Brown writing in *A Taste of Britain*, the first mention of these chewy discs was in 1760, when an apothecary in the West Yorkshire town, George Dunhill, added sugar to the juice of the local liquorice root. In 1893 there were eleven manufacturers of the Pontefract cake.

Rather beautiful, like seals of black wax, these discs still have enough of a following to keep at least one company in business, though I can't help feeling a little sad that they are no longer made with locally grown liquorice.

Bath Chaps

Hey ho, more flappy, dangly, wobbly bits sold as a delicacy. Bath chaps are in fact the cheeks from a long-jawed pig, such as the Gloucester Old Spot, and a speciality of that area. They are named after 'chops', as in the wobbly bits above your jaw ('Wipe the gravy off your chops,' my father used to say). They are boned, lightly brined, then cooked and moulded. Served dusted with breadcrumbs, usually pan-fried and eaten, as is much of this stuff, with mustard.

Fancy Toast

A sourdough loaf, with its slight acidity and chewy texture, makes very good breakfast material, though considered a bit modish by late adopters. Ciabatta is probably the least suitable, as the butter pours through the holes. Attempt it at your peril, though it is probably OK if there is no other bread in the house and you are wearing a very old dressing gown that already has the odd bit of marmalade on it anyway. Toasted malt loaf is in a class of its own, but delicious as it is – especially on a cold November morning – it has a distinct whiff of pension book about it.

White Food

From time to time my mother would make blancmange. For aesthetic reasons it had to be pink, though whether that was strawberry or cochineal mattered not, just so long as it wasn't white.

Blancmange – white food – is what she would put on the table when we tired of jelly with mandarin oranges set in it, or banana custard. (I'm not sure it is possible to tire of banana custard, but that is another matter.) Mum made hers by pouring boiled milk onto pale pink powder from a fat sachet and leaving it to set in the fridge. It was a treat, but then, anything set into the shape of a rabbit probably would have been seen as fun at that point in my life.

Had she made her blancmange the proper way, my poor mother would have had to set the warm milk with ingredients derived from the swim bladders of fish, or even ground antlers. Neither of which you could get at Percy Salt's grocery shop in Wolverhampton in 1964. But that pales into insignificance beside what a Norman cook would have had to do. According to historian Mary

Norwak, 'chicken flesh, picked into small pieces with a pin, mixed with whole boiled rice, almond milk and water. The surface would be sprinkled with little aniseed sweets or blanched almonds.' She then adds, without further comment, that 'a blancmange of fish was eaten on fast days'.

The day arrived when blancmange lost its savoury pretensions and took on a sweeter role: rosewater, sugar, aniseed, cream and almonds all took a turn to flavour the white food. By the early 1900s, fish bladders and stags' antlers had been lost to the newly arrived arrowroot, which was seen by some as debasing a grand dessert.

Blancmange, flummery, syllabub – why is it that so many English puddings sound like someone talking under water?

Golden Mint Humbugs

Humbugs, or at least the best of them, get their sharp corners from being cut from a long string of 'boiled and pulled' sugar, diagonally and with scissors. With its gay stripes, the humbug is thought of as typically Victorian (they had to get their jollies somewhere), yet it was probably developed from medieval cold cures, and is part of a long tradition of pulled sugar confections. The

Gibbs Golden Mint Humbug is the one shaped like a small jagged pyramid, the colour of honey with a satin-smooth coat.

Lardy Cake

A cake made from rendered pig fat, sugar and flour. How could one resist? If the recipe sounds unhealthy, unpalatable and eccentric, not to mention like frugality taken one step too far, then maybe we have to rethink what it is that makes food good to eat. Despite ticking every box in the shock-horror stakes, this cake manages to be one of the most agreeable things we can put in our mouths: soft, sweet, filling, and as comforting as hugging a well-padded aunt. In terms of filling an empty tummy, few things come close.

The spongy peel-and-currant-speckled cake hails from Wiltshire, which is of course pig-farming country, though it has been made throughout the land with slight variations. It is known in other counties as sharley cake, dripping cake or 'drips', and was almost certainly a food of the poor. Curiously, it is turned upside down to cool, to ensure that the fat runs back into the cake. The thin layer of grease that forms on your fingers, and more to the point, licking it off, is all part of the attraction.

Lardy cake is sliding into oblivion. In a decade it may have disappeared altogether, almost certainly because of its association with lard. Not that pig fat isn't delectable when used to add richness to a bread dough like this, but the American term 'lard-ass' is what springs into your mind every time you bite into this currant-speckled wonderloaf. Each chew brings with it a picture of wobbling butts in Lycra. The sort that look like two jellies in a pillowcase.

If you find the real thing (lardy cake that is, not a lard-ass), then take it home and eat it with a mug of strong tea. Enjoy it while you can; the clock is ticking for this little treasure.

The Expense Account Lunch

The expense account lunch isn't dead, just castrated.

The real big-bucks business in the City is done before most of us are out of bed. And while the striped-shirts-and-braces boys are trading just as frenetically as ever, their three-hour lunches accompanied by four-figure bottles of wine are just a distant memory. The 1980s was the high spot for the expense account lunch, complete with its 'Let's see how much we can spend' phenomenon. Since the crash of 1987, the hefty twice-yearly bonus is still with us, but the two-bottle-per-person lunch has had its wings clipped. The smoking ban hasn't helped. It is difficult to feel like a fat cat without a cigar in your mouth.

Business is business, and many meetings only achieve their goals when conducted over a plate of food. Clients seem more reasonable, their demands less exceptional, when they have something delicious in their mouths. It is not just about corporate hospitality. The truth of the matter is that it is simply harder to be unreasonable with a spoonful of bread and butter pudding melting on your tongue.

And bread and butter pudding it usually is. Most City high-flyers frequent smart restaurants where the food still contains a ghost of their boarding schools. The roast beef and spotted dick may have been given something of a makeover, but there is still a whiff of nanny about it. The accompanying bottles of Bollinger and Dom Perignon have not disappeared, but are consumed in somewhat less heroic quantities. The fact of the matter is that most expense account lunches now come with a side order of scrutiny, and every canapé and petit four must be justified.

The Suburban Day Out Lunch

Aunt Elvie needs a day out. She has the last will and testament, we have the car. It's an unspoken deal. It is worth helping her out of her seat, and then up the seven steps to the restaurant (one short step at a time, stopping for a break between each riser), to get the guilt off our shoulders. This is only the third time we have taken her out this year.

We drive to a pub that will later be thronged with the young and wannabe-young downing pints and Bacardi Breezers, but at lunchtime it is quiet, almost deathly so – there are just three couples in the place. All the men are wearing cardigans and ties, and judging by their hair the women have made slightly too much of an effort. The staff is appropriately welcoming, cheerful even, and the muzak is low enough not to worry Auntie, though she would probably appreciate Shirley Bassey's greatest hits if she could hear them.

The tables are as polished as the carpet is swirly, the horse-brasses are shining, the fire has even been lit, though on close inspection it turns out to be one of those gas-fed efforts that need no stacking or raking out. We order a shandy and a lemonade and lime. Auntie has a small sherry the colour of a mahogany commode. The menu is partly on laminated paper, partly on a blackboard proudly announcing Today's Specials, which are, one suspects, the same as yesterday's specials.

There is home-made soup, though of what we're not told, roast chicken or beef with 'all the trimmings', grilled lamb cutlets, and fillet of plaice either grilled or deep-fried with lemon. Someone has rubbed out the first and last letters from the 'trimmings', so what we are actually offered in the genteel delights of this suburban public house is roast beef and rimming, but I'm the only one who seems to understand, or indeed even to notice.

I toy with the idea of ordering the vegetarian lasagne for a main course, but think better of it, the word 'roast' being a temptation too great to pass up in favour of something from a frozen catering-food supplier. My aunt peruses the menu and says how nice it all sounds, but we know she says it only to underline how much she appreciates the chance of looking at a menu at all. She has known she would order the grilled plaice since the alarm on the Teasmade went off this morning.

They make a bit of a fuss of bringing round the bread rolls, which are somehow neither white nor brown but something between the two, making much of the word warm, as in 'Would anyone like a *warm* bread roll?' Having taken a roll, I then find that the soup (vegetable, as it happens) comes with a roll on the side, so I now have two warm, neither brown nor white rolls to deal with.

The meal goes on like this, with the occasional 'It's always nice here, isn't it?' or 'Have they changed those curtains since we were here last?', for an interminable two hours, dawdling through pieces of plaice the size of kites and some rather good chips. The garnish is peas, of course, half a tomato and some cress. We finish with 'home-made' pie and custard and a crème caramel. On being asked if we are paying by credit card, my aunt pipes up snappily, 'Cash, we don't need any credit, thank you,' totally misunderstanding the point of American Express.

We then take another age to get down the steps, after a fifteen-minute trip to the loo where she only powders her nose anyway, and slowly drive off home. On the way my aunt says how she wishes we could do this more often. 'Yes, let's,' I say with as much enthusiasm as I can muster. 'Yes, let's.'

Quality Street

Leave an open box of Quality Street in a room, and even the faddiest chocolate connoisseur will probably have nicked one by the time you come back. Even if you can resist the assortment of the, frankly rather sweet, chocolate toffees and fondants themselves, there is much pleasure to be had in simply rustling through the box. Most people I know claim only to like the green-foil-covered triangles, with their faint taste of praline, but I think they are fibbing. Quality Street, with its humpy purple caramel Brazils, round strawberry creams and chocolate-coated toffees, remains strangely unbowed by the move towards fine chocolate.

It may well be the bright reds and yellows of the cellophane wrappings (the foil is always silver, only the cellophane is coloured) that appeal, or it may simply be that they bring back memories of childhood Christmases. Either way, they remain a steady favourite. It is easy to see why. Rolling the coin-like, gold-wrapped cream toffee over and over with your tongue is one of the enduring pleasures of life, especially when it clonks against the roof of your mouth. Quality Street also remain the only chocolates on earth that audibly squeak as you unwrap them.

Branston Pickle

Despite the heroic work of Britain's unstoppable band of pickle-makers who sell their hand-made, ruby-and-amber-coloured wares at farm shops, delis and country fairs, Branston is what most Brits mean when they say pickle. Twenty-eight million jars of this dark, sticky and faintly sinister-looking condiment are purchased each year. Its manufacturers advise that their mud-hued, syrupy tracklement sits well with burgers and hot dogs, yet in truth most of it will find its way into cheese sandwiches. One can only imagine what the Italians would make of the makers' suggestion that it also goes well with pizza.

The recipe is secret (if only), and Crosse & Blackwell – who have made the much-loved accompaniment since 1922 – insist its enduring success is due to the distinctive mixture of sweetness and tang. They have recently introduced a smooth version, which has the curious characteristic of having no lumps, presumably a pickle for people who don't really like pickle.

Pickling is part of our country-cooks' heritage, and the craft of mixing crunchy, lightly cooked vegetables in a sweet-sour sauce is one to which other nations' cooks can only aspire. Green tomatoes, cucumber, onions and garlic are simmered each autumn with vinegar, coriander seed, allspice, cardamom, cumin, cinnamon and occasionally turmeric to give a variety of spiced relishes that manage to bring to life everything from cold roast meats to grilled mackerel, and are an integral part of a ploughman's lunch. The flavours are bold, sweet and sharp, yet each inevitably secret recipe relies upon subtle and carefully considered spicing. The colours range from brightest purple to mustard yellow, and despite the rich, thick sauce that binds them together, many of the ingredients are instantly recognisable for what they are.

Set side by side with these masterpieces of the pickle-maker's art, a jar of Branston, especially if the rim of the jar is encrusted with old drips, as it so often is, might appear crude; yet it cannot be for nothing that one in three British households has some in the cupboard. Branston has fingered exactly the attributes of pickle that we appear to appreciate: a regular, somewhat monotone sharpness, a dark sticky sweetness and, perhaps above all, few bits. Strangely, it is the 'bits' that true pickle is all about. Despite lacking the bright colour, recognisable vegetables, spices and excitement of the home-made version, Branston is a condiment to which the British are deeply attached. Whether it is a pickle in the traditional sense is territory onto which I shall not trespass.

Paying the Price

You learn to arm yourself with a good, flat-bottomed bag with strong handles. Strawberries and redcurrants tend to come in open punnets that will spill amongst the spinach and work their way down to the bottom of your plastic bag if you don't. The smell of warm raspberries that wafts up from your shopping on the way home is actually six quid's worth turning to jam in your bag.

You queue like a true Brit and hand over your money. There's a lot of crestfallen clattering in the cash box, followed by a hopeful look on the farmer's face. 'I don't suppose . . . ?' It is part of the deal that stallholders never have enough change. Just as it is that the people who shop in such places always seem only to have twenty-quid notes. Go with bulging pockets rather than a fat wallet. A farmers' market is the only place where you can offload your week's coppers and get a smile in return.

A Third-Generation Fishmonger

I have been a customer of Mr Hatt's for almost twenty years. There is nothing in his shop – it's more of a stall really – that isn't first-class, spanking fresh and smelling of the sea. It is to him, a third-generation fishmonger, that I turn for a pair of red mullet for baking with olives and thyme, a bag of mussels for steaming till their shells gape lapis blue, or a cod flap for the cat's tea. It is here I go for slices of smoked salmon and whole golden mackerel, for a majestic cooked crab or a dozen native oysters on the shell. You can't go wrong at Mr Hatt's.

At one time every town had a friendly fishmonger, if not two. But since the eighties they have gone down like flies, and they are now as rare as ironmongers. It was

MacFisheries that started the downturn in 1983 when they decided to close all their retail shops. Most towns on this sea-surrounded land are now left without anywhere in which to buy a kipper.

The Work of Pixies

You arrive early, stand in a short excitable line that, rather than annoying you the way it might at the post office, gives you instead time to leisurely peruse the produce on display. The ageing wicker hampers filled with bunches of spinach as bright as a button; faded hessian sacks of flaky-skinned potatoes so freshly dug their soil still has the odd live worm sticking to it; a wooden bowl of cucumbers no bigger than courgettes. There are young nettles for soup, white celery with dark soil clinging to its ribs, and rose-pink radishes with snow-white tips. To your left is an old wooden crate with young, purple garlic, each bunch secured with purple string; another with summer cabbages whose leaves end at a sharp point like a minaret; beetroots the size of golf balls. You spot peas for popping, broad beans no bigger than your little fingernail, lettuces heavy with heart leaves and milky sap on their cut stems.

Suddenly your eyes settle on a shallow cane basket,

heavily weathered, its fine weave fraying and split. Filled with orange, vermilion and green tomatoes, some round or shaped like baubles, others daubed with yellow smudges or streaks of green, each one ridged and gnarled. You would need a heart of steel not to dip your hand in, and tastebuds to match.

This is not a pipe dream, the imagination of a frustrated townie getting carried away, a food writer trying to sell you the idea of shopping at a farmers' market. It is the Fern Verrow stall at Borough Market in London on a Saturday morning in July. It is as you might imagine a vegetable stall run by pixies, who get up each morning before dawn to tend their baby pumpkins and climb up beanstalks. Yet it is as real as any greengrocer, a tiny, magical place you wish existed in every town, if not on every street corner.

Gravy

When I was in need of my mother's apron strings I would stand and watch her making gravy. Setting the roast itself to one side under a bit of foil, she would put the roasting tin, charred black with the deposits of a married lifetime of Sunday lunches, onto the hob. She would add a spoonful of Bisto, then slowly pour boiling water, usually from the veggies, into the tin. Pouring and stirring with her wooden spoon at the same time, she would scrape away at the crusty, roasted bits stuck to the bottom of the pan, letting them dissolve in the gravy. I don't know why she added the Bisto. The gravy would have been fine without it. I think everyone did in those days. At Christmas she would add a drop of sherry, and everyone would make the same joke year after year about getting tiddly from the gravy.

Gravy divides the nation. You either like it thick or thin. By thin I mean unthickened, rather than lacking in body. Most gravy in this country has too much body, by which I generally mean an overdose of flour, or the inclusion of gravy granules. The point of gravy is not only to lubricate and moisten, but also to bring the disparate ingredients together on the plate. It has a uniting effect, acting as any good host should, getting the potatoes, green vegetables and accompaniments to know one another, and even hold hands.

Thick gravy can be a bit of a thug, and is inclined to overpower everything else on the plate. It is also thought by some to be a bit common, but it is very welcome with sausages, fried chicken, liver and, in my book, bubble and squeak. Thin gravy tends to be more flattering to the meat and has a truer flavour, though it must be said that it is distinctly less comforting.

Thick gravy adds a luscious quality to meat, a voluptu-ousness, a smoothness and suavity. It soothes the mouth, softens the blow of horseradish or mustard, coats the tongue and provides a blanket of savour for meat and vegetables alike. Thin gravy, that is, the encrusted juices of the meat dissolved in water, wine or stock, wets the meat without altering its character, and looks more elegant and simple on the plate. It has an integrity, a purity and a point to it which are lacking in the thick stuff. However, it is less satisfying, and is more welcome in summer than in winter.

The essence of gravy is that it holds within it the heart and soul of the meat. The sugars present in the juices that have escaped as the meat roasts automatically caramelise in the pan. Gravy seeks to exploit the deep savour and *umami* contained in those burnt-on juices. Water, stock or wine will release the goodness (I like to think of this as the meat's spirit) and trapped flavour, which is why it is essential to scrape as you stir, and why a flat-edged wooden spoon is such a successful gravy-making tool. Adding flour or a Bisto-style product effectively introduces an outside presence into the finished product, destroying in one stroke (or several stirs) the purity of the juices.

The Extravagant Cook

It is usually men who go mad in the butcher's. Asking, in less than discreet tones, for a large rib of beef, for the two thickest pork chops and, almost as an afterthought, a piece of fillet steak. 'Oh, and some sausages for breakfast.' Which is fine, until you know that their wife only sent them out for a pound of economy mince. Further, that they never have anything but Weetabix for breakfast.

Men tend to show off in food shops in a way women don't. Two men, finding themselves at the deli counter at the same time, will act as if they are side by side at the traffic lights, each one revving up while surreptitiously eyeing the other's vehicle (in this case the BMW and the Audi have been temporarily swapped for wire baskets).

The extravagant shopper buys not with any great knowledge or expertise, or even with any common sense, but with an eye for the most expensive, exclusive and unusual. This is the shopper who buys olive oil that is three times the price of the best in your cupboard, who picks up the large pack of saffron, the truffle in the jar. Truth is, he wouldn't know a truffle from a dog turd, but that's not the point. Furthermore, he wouldn't know if the risotto even has truffle in it, but he wants to be seen buying one, especially when being watched by another male.

The extravagant shopper is the one who has a fridge full of stuff but doesn't know what to do with it. Like the television that cost him as much as a car, and that he doesn't know how to use, or the expensive, abandoned gym membership. It's not what you have in your shopping basket that's important, but how much it cost.

A dinner party with the extravagant shopper is a non-stop exhibition of ego-cooking. The best ingredients, the flashiest recipes and, actually, quite sound cooking, albeit done on a cooker that wouldn't look out of place at Gordon Ramsay's. It's the culinary equivalent of driving a Porsche Cayenne.

That Old Black Magic

On Fridays, my father would bring home a box of chocolates for my mother. Usually it was Milk Tray or Dairy Box, the latter lacking the delectable little lime barrel that I loved more than any other chocolate. From time to time he would be holding a box of Terry's All Gold instead, a more upmarket dark chocolate assortment that we usually gave as presents at Christmas or if we were repaying a favour.

It seemed, at least to a boy aged eight, that there were different boxes of chocolates for different occasions. I could gauge my father's state of mind by which assortment he brought home:

Milk Tray – Produced at odd times during the week for no apparent reason. Like apples and onions, they were something we usually had in the house.

Dairy Box – My father would buy this milky selection for himself as much as for anyone else. He adored the soft nougat and praline centres. The appearance of Dairy Box usually coincided with him being in a bad mood. This particular treat was his personal teddy bear, and made him feel better about life. It was what I always gave him for Father's Day.

Terry's All Gold – The chocolates for 'special occasions' and for presents. The one shaped like a mandarin orange was my favourite, but it was rarely still in place once the box got round to me. In the days before luxury chocolate shops, All Gold was as posh as it got, unless you were the sort of person who bought Bendicks or Elizabeth Shaw, which my father would have thought a tad over the top.

Weekend – A rather cheap and brassy assortment of fondants, marzipans and brightly coloured fudges that the old man would always buy for my stepmother. Even at the tender age of twelve I thought of these as sweets rather than chocolates. I remember turning my nose up at them once, with a particularly Fanny Cradock sort of *hauteur*. 'Sometimes, Nigel,' snapped my father, 'you behave like the Queen of Sheba.'

After Eight Mints – It must be Christmas. My father would become apoplectic with rage if anyone put an empty wrapper back in the box.

Selection boxes – (Again, must be Christmas.) At school we believed these Christmas stalwarts were where the manufacturers used up the out-of-date chocolate bars, partly because everything in a selection box, especially those ones shaped like Christmas stockings, always tasted slightly stale. Not that it stopped the selection box being one of the best bits of Christmas. Anyway, I have yet to eat a finger of fudge that didn't taste as if it was made ten years ago. For some reason that is part of their charm.

Brawn and Mustard

Brawn – that dish of cured pork set in firm jelly – is probably not at the top of the average bear's must-eat list, though it certainly has its fans. A speciality of the South-West, it is served almost without fail with a smear of hot yellow mustard, presumably to help you get it down. Cold jellied meat is currently about as unfashionable as any food could possibly be, and indeed it would be hard to find anyone under the age of fifty who would give it house room. It might help if this recipe was as pretty as the classic French jambon persillé, with its marbling of pink meat and fresh, green-flecked jelly. Sadly, the British offering is generally dull beige-brown or orange-red. Either way, it's not much of a looker.

Yet brawn is frugal, ingenious and tasty. I'm not sure why there should be anything wrong with eating a dish of boiled, boned and pressed pig's head set in jelly made from its own feet. But somehow there just is. Maybe it's because I always think I am going to come across a toenail, or perhaps an eyeball winking at me from the jelly.

Trifle – A Social Indicator

Layer after layer of frivolity. Is there anything quite so heavenly as the deep, cool luxury of a home-made trifle? (It is what I imagine angels eat when they are not practising the harp.) The thick layers of wine-sodden sponge cake, soft ripe fruit, thick custard and whipped cream, and the brittle crunch of toasted almonds are as near as one could imagine to paradise. If the word 'trifle' is supposed to mean something of little consequence, then we have christened this pudding inaccurately. It is probably our most important and celebrated dessert, next to Christmas pudding. Yet few recipes in recent years have been so travestied, cheapened and embarrassed. What can be a glorious orgy of joyful voluptuousness is all too often not worthy of the name.

We seem to have always had trifles, but they actually hail from 1751, when Hannah Glasse published the fourth edition of her book *The Art of Cookery Made Plain and Easy*. While there had been earlier recipes of the same name, this was the first time anyone mentioned dunking sponge (in her case brioche) into the custard. Previously set with rennet and resembling a rosewater-scented junket, trifle then had not only a layer of sponge and jam, but an element of frivolity too, in the form of 'sweetmeats according to your fancy'. After an austere start as a simple set custard, the trifle as we know it was starting to take shape.

I take trifle seriously – perhaps a bit more seriously than anyone should. But it is a habit that runs in our family, though I baulk at including a layer of jelly as my father did. A typical recipe of the late 1700s would include ratafia biscuits, sherry and a layer of syllabub made with cream and orange juice. You might find embellishments of rosewater, cinnamon, redcurrant jelly, gooseberries and vanilla, but there is unlikely to be a glacé cherry in sight. By the mid-1900s, scores of recipes were being published – trifle was enjoying something of a heyday, the lemon tart of its day – and our party piece had formed itself into layers of sponge or macaroons soaked in sherry and white wine, a layer of custard, followed by another of lemon and orange syllabub, then a final one of whipped cream. Dreamy, yes, possibly even the food of angels, but with little in the way of the essential frivolity, such as a scattering of crystallised violets and rose petals, or maybe candied orange peel.

After the war, the cake was often swapped for bread, but the real crimes were committed a decade or so later, not out of necessity, but in the name of modernism. As was so often the case, it was the 1960s that were particularly harsh on this classic, and layers of jelly, tinned apricots, 'hundreds and thousands' and, perhaps most humiliating of all, teeth-shattering silver balls, made an appearance. Once gracing our tables like a favourite and slightly tiddly old aunt, our cherished party dessert now resembled nothing more than an old tart in a leopardskin coat.

To complete the fall from grace, the 1970s saw this formerly proud pudding in its death throes. A packet of 'Quick Trifle', complete with custard powder, fake cream and a layer of multicoloured sugar sprinkles, meant that an instant version could be on the table in a matter of minutes. Forget the hand-churned, vanilla-scented syllabub, the rose petals glistening with sugar and the thick layer of billowing cream, this brightly coloured impostor with its layer of red jelly was embraced by the busy housewife with the same gusto with which she had adopted instant coffee and white sliced bread. Stripped of so many of her decadent layers, our tipsy aunt had gone from simply having her hat on skew-whiff, to being caught without any knickers.

By the late 1970s our celebration dessert had become, at least in Middle England, an assembly of trifle sponges soaked in sherry, with a layer of red or orange jelly, another of Bird's custard and a topping of whipped cream. If fruit was involved, it would mainly be something from a tin – mandarin oranges when children were to be present, apricots for a party, with peaches in syrup coming out at Christmas. Trifle sponges, like Vesta curries or Surprise peas, were among the science-enhanced curiosities of the modern cook's world: brittle bricks of dried sponge cake that swelled into soft, tender cake with the application of a little sherry.

Unwittingly, a glass bowl of custard and cream had become as clear an indicator of your position in society as the newspaper you read. Was the sherry you doused your sponges with Emva Cream (the *Express*), Harvey's Bristol Cream (the *Daily Mail*) or Croft Original (the *Telegraph*)? Was jelly present, and if so was it strawberry or orange, Rowntree's or Chivers, and was your cream fresh, or from a tin? Every layer put us in our place.

The most telling giveaway, though, is the final arrangement of miniature sweetmeats on the top, glacé cherries, toasted almonds and diamonds of green angelica being further up the social ladder than, say, silver balls or multicoloured sugar strands. Sugar flower petals show delicacy and tenderness, yellow mimosa sugar balls a certain lightness of spirit, piping-bag swirls of cream are a touch Hyacinth Bucket. The most beautiful way to finish off is with a perfectly smooth blanket of whipped cream, without a sugar-dipped frivolity in sight. But then it wouldn't be trifle. Our favourite celebration dessert simply wouldn't live down to its name.

The Best Biscuit of All?

I cannot go any further without mentioning my favourite biscuit of all time, now sadly, tragically, extinct. The oaty, crumbly, demerara notes of the long-forgotten Abbey Crunch will remain forever on my lips. I loved this biscuit as much as anything I have ever eaten, and often, in moments of solitude, I still think about its warm, buttery, sugary self. My guess is that as well as the butter and the brown sugar it also had a goodly bit of salt in it, which is why it tasted so damn good. It's gone, and I really should move on, but it breaks my heart that it has been replaced by the over-sweet, chaff-like Hob Nob, which is frankly a very poor replacement.

And just when I thought no one else remembered this biscuit, and that I alone pined for its open-textured sugariness, I found both a website and a book whose authors feel the same. I sense an appreciation society coming on, if not the annual laying of a wreath.

Chocolate Limes

A bit of an anorak's sweet, this one. Crunchy, opaque, lime-flavoured coating hiding a core of soft chocolate. Probably enjoyed by those who used to like the lime barrel in Cadbury's Dairy Box, it is an unusual, though far from unsuccessful, pairing. Gerard Coleman at L'Artisan du Chocolat, the pinnacle of the chocolate-maker's art, makes a tiny jewel of a chocolate containing the zest of the lumi – the Middle Eastern dried lime – which is probably like comparing Shostakovich to Girls Aloud.

Sharing the Bill – The Weasel at the Table

You have had a good time, shared confidences, the mood is buoyant and the decibel level just the right side of intrusive. You chose well, had plenty to drink, but no more than anyone else at the table, and feel for once that you managed to include everyone in the conversation. All things considered, especially knowing how tables for eight can go so hideously wrong, you declare the evening a sweeping success. Add to that the odd scrap of delectable gossip you overheard, and you are wondering why you don't do this more often.

The bill arrives. A clatter of plastic is thrown at the plate, a system of splitting the cost that drives the waiting staff nuts, but works well for the diners, and a few others throw in a handful of cash. Someone grabs the notes and says to the waitress, 'Put two-eighths on my card, will you? I need the cash.' Apart from the harassed staff, everything seems smooth enough.

And then you hear it, a little squeak from somewhere further down the table, the words you thought were only heard at other people's tables. Apologetic, disgruntled, dogmatic, and with an immovable quality that brings the jollity and easiness to a resounding halt. 'Actually, I didn't have a starter, and I didn't really drink anything. Here's a cheque for what I had.' The one, lone diner amongst your jolly, sharing, caring party who has kept a tally of the exact amount she owes. While you were laughing loudly about that incident in Phuket, and half-listening to your ex discussing your intimate details with her mate, someone was mentally tallying up her exact share of the bill, to the penny. Suddenly you realise that you never really spoke to her either, and nor are you sure who it was who invited her.

The bill-pedant is the unexpected shower at the village fête, the downstairs neighbour who bangs on his ceiling at midnight to get you keep the noise down, the man who not only keeps all his receipts but files them. This the person who reported her neighbour during the hosepipe ban, the one who leaves notes to remind everyone to lock the door behind them when they go out.

And now she's at your table, demanding to pay only for what she consumed. If it was a man you could laugh it off by calling him a tight-arse and taking the piss out of him. But to do it to this quiet, mouse-like creature at the end of the table would seem like bullying. It doesn't dawn on you that it is she who is the big bad bully.

You could tell the waitress to put the shortfall on your own credit card, but to do so would look condescending, and would embarrass Little Miss Moth-Wallet even more. But then, as she has already managed to embarrass herself so much already, surely she could handle it. You wish everyone would just laugh and pay her share, but then it dawns on you that your meal with friends and their friends was never what it seemed. All along there was someone who shouldn't have been there, who would have been better off eating on her own. You feel cheated. Two minutes ago your world had seemed such a generous and bountiful and good-natured place, and now you have been brought down to earth with a bump. No matter how good that grilled rabbit with mustard and pancetta was, how velvety the Pinot Noir, you have been left with a bad taste in your mouth to go home with. The bill-pedant has struck.

Sweetness and Light

It was John Tovey who taught me to make scones, at his country-house hotel Miller Howe, with its magnificent view of what he insisted on calling The English Lakes. One can only assume the name Windermere smacked a little too much of bank-holiday charabanc trips and fish-and-chip teas. It was John, or Mr T as he preferred to be known, who insisted that his young trainee cook gaze out of the window at the daffodils shuddering in the spring breeze, and the calm waters of the lake beyond, as he rubbed the fridge-cold butter into the flour with his fingertips. He demanded that you lift the ingredients a good two feet above the bowl and let them slip lightly through your fingers, presumably taking air with them as they fell. His reasoning was that 'A light heart makes for light baking, lad.' I thought his method something of an affectation at the time (the hotel had a collection of gilt cherubs hanging on invisible wires from the ceiling), yet I have grown to agree with him. I have yet to meet a grouch who can make a decent cake.

Scones on Harris

'You'll be back for your tea? I serve it at nine,' announced Mrs Dodie, our white-haired landlady, as we left her little Scottish farm for a pub supper. Nine seemed an odd time to indulge in tea and scones, yet that is exactly what we were expected to do. Unsure whether this was a quaint local habit or simply a ruse to get her two young backpackers home before they had time to get bladdered, we nevertheless made the most of the wobbly trolley of feather-light oatmeal scones and the brown pot of strong tea that she wheeled into her silent, neat front room on the dot of nine. While it saved two broke teenagers the expense of a pudding in the pub, Mrs Dodie's tea left us with little alternative other than to take an early night and drink our smuggled-in miniatures of malt whisky under our threadbare candlewick bedspreads.

PG Tips

PG Tips is where most tea-drinkers start, and where millions of them stay. For all our connections with India and its shade-grown teas of infinite delicacy and gentle charm, we seem as a nation to have developed a preference for teas that hit us over the head. Strong, loud and lacking in subtlety, PG Tips isn't referred to as builders' tea for nothing.

PG is a mug tea, blended for drinking in copious quantities to quench a thirst, or for dunking a biscuit. It responds well to milk and sugar, and what it lacks in subtlety, it makes up for in bold, in-your-face flavour as an all-round family tea.

PG Tips will always be associated with the monkeys who were used to advertise it. Dressed up in a variety of loud costumes and placed in slapstick scenarios, the group of chattering chimps appeared as the product's commercial face for many years. My father insisted I looked like one particular chimp, which with my big ears and half-crown haircut I probably did. We became fond of them in much the same way as we became attached to actors in our favourite soap. And while many of us have moved on to experience the superior teas of small estates with their fine, understated characters and jewel-like purity, most of us will admit to keeping a few bags of PG in the cupboard, if only for when we need something a little stronger, or when the plumber needs a mug of tea and a slice of fruitcake.

When the worst has happened, and a kind Samaritan offers to make a pot of tea, it is PG Tips to which they refer, and not anything more subtle. PG Tips is life's cure-all, a hug in a mug.

Robertson's Golden Shred

I'm ten, and I offer to put marmalade on my dad's toast. The more I can get him to eat, the nearer I am to getting another golly badge.

The golly badge, modelled on the hero of Frances and Bertha Upton's 1895 book *Two Dutch Dolls*, was what you got for collecting ten of the paper gollies that were tucked very tightly behind the label of each pot of Golden Shred. Robertson's, who manufacture the famous amber-coloured preserve, had found a way of securing the tokens so they couldn't be pulled out from the jars on the supermarket shelves by light-fingered collectors. Soldiers, sailors, footballers, racing drivers, policemen – you name it, there was a golly badge for every career, sport and hobby. There was even one dressed as an air stewardess, which would surely make her a trolley-dolly golly. I had enough to go up both lapels of my school blazer, though not quite as many as Paul Gripton.

Of course the golly has now gone, swept away on a tide of political correctness (though the manufacturers cite other reasons), but the badges live on as collectors' items. Had they continued, Robertson's would probably have been forced by those who read the Society pages of the *Guardian* to have extended the collection to include a disabled golly, a hearing-impaired golly, an obese (sorry, circumferentially-challenged) golly, and of course a lesbian and a cross-gender golly too. The fact that golly had been a transvestite for years seemed to go unnoticed. Just check out the one in the nurse's uniform if you don't believe me. One glimpse at one of the many golly websites will bring back memories of the much-loved badges long lost or swapped for a packet of Woodbines.

At one point in its history, the now controversial badges somewhat overshadowed the marmalade itself. But those who like more quiver than peel, and who prefer their preserves sweet rather than bitter, and therefore possibly don't really like marmalade at all, may well appreciate a dollop of Golden Shred on their breakfast toast.

The Specialist Shop

Patron-owned businesses that specialise in one type of food have been around since long before the first butcher donned his stripy apron. So it is sad that greengrocers, fishmongers and even local chemists are now almost a rare breed. In my own small area of London we have lost two butchers and a greengrocer in three years. I wonder whether the ones who remain do so only because they either own their freehold or are on a peppercorn rent.

What hits you about the small specialist shops that have survived is that for the most part they are good of their kind, innovative, clean, well-stocked and open long hours. My local fishmonger opens before eight, as do the greengrocer and the butcher. It was generally the also-rans that were forced to close. If someone does something well, with passion, vision and an encyclopaedic knowledge of what they are selling, they stand a much better chance of survival.

If we are turning back to those that remain of our local, specialist shops, it is partly because our own knowledge of food is greater than it was. We have become suspicious of big agri-business and food retailing. We want to buy our cheese, bread, pastries and fish from someone who can provide something a little more interesting than the major players – a cheese from a small farm in the mountains, a shoulder of pork from a rare pig that has been bred for flavour and succulence rather than yield, a fish that was landed that morning rather than a week ago and that has had to dawdle through the food chain. It is less to do with rarefied tastes, an escape from the everyday, the ordinary and the OK, than with finding ingredients that add up to making a meal that is a joy on every level, from buying it to taking it hot and sizzling from the oven.

The Case for Clicks not Bricks

Where internet shopping wins hands down is in giving us the opportunity to have the selection and value for money that a supermarket can offer without the trauma of parking the car, extricating a trolley from its mate, and playing the endlessly amusing 'Is that line moving quicker than ours?' game while waiting to be relieved of our money. It can save us from witnessing the twenty-stone shopper whose trolley is piled up with enough crisps, buns and pop to stock a school tuck shop for a week, from being subjected to coma-inducing piped muzak, and finally from the humiliation of having our charge card refused in public. But best of all it means that no longer do we have to be asked, for the 150th time, if we have a bloody loyalty card.

The internet allows us to sit in the cool comfort of our own home or office, glass of wine at our side, clicking our ergonomically-designed mouse instead of doing battle with bags, boxes and pin numbers. Our shopping can be delivered in hourly time slots. It can take that long to get into Sainsbury's car park. Early adopters, that well-educated, confident, open-to-change social group that started shopping for food on the internet years before anyone else, now do it so regularly that it is as natural as opening a book. Even those normally distrusting of technology, whose comfort zone is the thought of Big Brother reading the minute details of their shopping lists in order to keep files about them, are now taking up the opportunity to shop from their armchairs. At least it gives them something to do when the adverts are on. Pity that in doing so we have managed to see off that village shop we loved so much.

And so to the avocado page. Do we go for the individual crocodile-skinned Hass, the organic two-pack, the single large green (as if there's any other colour) or the perennially doubtful 'ripe and ready to eat'? If we had them in front of us we could make our decision in a split second. Peering at a stamp-sized thumbnail picture of a pear-shaped fruit on a screen offers little or no help. When we shop for food, the smell, look and feel of the ingredients is all part of the deal. Apart from the sheer tactile pleasure, it is often what makes us plump for one thing rather than another. The feel of an avocado, the scent of a mango, the crustiness of a white loaf are what help us make the right decisions. But then, some people have met their other half over the internet.

Frying Tonight

You file impatiently back up the carpeted stairs, past the usherettes with their beehive hairdos and the popcorn booth, and through the foyer. You go down the steps and past the long and somewhat inebriated queue for the late-night show. Your pace gradually quickens. Having safely left the rest of the audience behind, you join the short queue at the fish-and-chip shop, pull your collar up to keep out the cold, and then wait for what seems like forever to get to the counter.

People walk past clutching their haddock and chips. You can smell the warm paper, the piercing vinegar, and can almost taste the salty batter. Your breath forms clouds in the frosty night air. You rub your hands together. You wait, and you wait.

Finally you get your hands on your own hot parcel. You find a wall to sit on, and peel back the white paper. The batter is still crisp, the fish comes away in thick, chalk-white flakes. You inhale what seems to be, for that moment in the cold night air, the most perfect smell in the world. A smell steeped in history, gluttony and national pride. A smell to beat off all comers – the garlic notes of the stir-fry, the soft dough-n-cheese scent of the pizza, the warm, wet-lettuce aroma of the Big Mac. Waves of heat, acid, salt and ozone rise in a cloud into the frost-etched air. A perfect moment.

Visitors from abroad, and indeed anyone born less than fifteen years ago, must wonder how the inhabitants of this country earned their reputation as such consummate lovers of fish and chips. Even now one assumes there is a friendly chippy frying tonight on every corner, even though it was probably long ago replaced by a branch of Starbucks.

Those that have survived are either the best of their kind, serving fresh fish in light-as-a-feather batter and hand-cut chips to a discerning, grateful clientele, or have diversified to offer a little Chinese on the side. It is almost impossible to find a seriously good chippy in London's West End, so the classic British night out of a film followed by fish and chips eaten from the paper is something easier done by the seaside.

It is of course purely coincidental that the decline of the chippy started around the same time they stopped wrapping our cod and chips in old newspaper. We can't blame the health inspectors for everything, but certainly some magic was lost once your chips no longer came with something to read. The smell of hot, greasy news-print is perhaps the best seasoning a fish can have.

The fish-and-chip business has had more bad luck thrown at it than seems fair. The emergence of the burger bars and kebab shops, the massive rise in high-street rates that have seen off all but the biggest retailing names, the health lobby and now, to cap it all, the nation's dwindling fish stocks. It's a wonder any are still in business.

Those who peddle frozen fish clad in batter as thick as their shop's Formica counter tops, with jars of sad pickled eggs and a lone, armour-plated saveloy waiting patiently for someone drunk enough to order it, are still around. They exist out of necessity. During the day they provide cheap(ish) sustenance to those who cannot cook. At night they are a safe harbour for anyone who has drunk enough not to care what they put in their mouth.

It is difficult to know whether the fish and chip is on the brink of extinction or a comeback. Some enterprising soul may well see the gaping hole that has appeared in the takeaway food market. But what form should our fish-and-chip suppers take in the twenty-first century? We have much to learn from the Japanese, with their gossamer-thin tempura batter. Could a lighter coating, barely strong enough to hold the fish, be the future for the fish-and-chip trade? At least that would appease the health police. Should we rethink the thick, greasy chips, and offer something more delicate and infinitely crisp?

Or should we simply leave it be, and hope that the few that have survived so far always will? As I write, my local chippy has just gone out of business.

The Italians have their feather-light zucchini flowers, the French their frites, the Spanish their cloud-like churros (which they then go on to soak in hot chocolate), and the Indians have pans full of crackling hot samosas. Snacks and vegetables, starters and side dishes, the world's kitchens are full of food that has seen the inside of a pan full of deep, golden oil, but surely the British are the only ones so far to deep-fry one of their national dishes.

The Taste of the New

Historically, the British roast and boil their meat, though in the last decade we have also embraced the grill so beloved of the cooks of southern Europe, Asia and the United States. About time. One should thank the River Café, whose bold, idiosyncratic way with meat on the grill has slowly percolated through the restaurant business to our own plates at home. Our meat is now scorched in appetisingly black stripes, the fat golden, the flesh singed from the bars of the grill. We have added charcoal to our national seasonings of salt and pepper.

The Grow-Your-Own Cook

The root vegetables are planted with the moon, beans in the second quarter, salad leaves in the first. The kids have made a scarecrow for the allotment with the face of George Bush cut from the *Guardian*, and the sunflowers are left over winter to feed the birds. The grow-your-own cook is a committed recycler, compost-maker and seed-sower, a plastic-bag refusenik and a passionate family cook. No meal is better than one for which they have grown the main ingredient themselves, a mantra which they live by, especially in the autumn when their allotment becomes bountiful.

They understand the unity of growing, cooking and eating, and have experienced for themselves the pleasure, total and complete, that is eating something you have grown from seed. Their pots are old and mismatched and have cooked a thousand good meals; their knives and forks were their grandmothers', and every ingredient in the kitchen is organic or free-range or made by a tousle-haired artisan. The farmers' market and the wholefood store – they go on their bikes – are their answer to the corner shop and the supermarket, a place they hate and will use only when they have to.

There is a lot of yoghurt consumed in this kitchen, and home-made bread and Neal's Yard-type cheeses too. The kids are used to the lack of sweets and to eating a carrot instead of the longed-for Mars bar, and love making Jack o' lanterns out of the interminable pumpkins that come in from the garden. They may be only eight and five, but they know their rocket from their kale, and can move a ladybird from a wall to a black-fly-infested broad bean plant without hurting it.

This is a proper baker's kitchen, with something always in the oven, though it is difficult to time things accurately on a wood-burning stove. The kids are everything, and the main reason that so much time is spent planting, hoeing, weeding, watering. It is all for them. One can only hope they will still thank Mum and Dad for their names, so cool and wacky at five or eight years of age, when they go for their first job.

Pre-Jamie Man

A wooden spoon is an affront to a man's masculinity. Cooking is 'women's work', unless you are talking about professional chefs, which is another matter altogether (it's hot and hard and heavy and, like football, is all about teamwork). Men, if they are true men, wouldn't dream of baking a cake or carrying a shopping basket.

The more enlightened, unthreatened male might cook once a year. The Great Dish will be made to his special recipe, a secret of course, but will usually involve rather a lot of Tabasco sauce. There will be much noise and mess, everyone else will be banned from entering the kitchen. There will be clattering and banging, cursing and harrumphing, testing and tasting. Whatever happens, it is unlikely you will see supper this side of nine o'clock.

It will be an event. The meal must be praised in glowing terms by all concerned, both at the time and at every possible opportunity throughout the coming year. What must not be mentioned is the record-breaking amount of washing up The Great Dish produces (it is a man's unquestionable right to use every piece of kitchen equipment available). To suggest that The Great Dish may need a pinch more salt or pepper, a tad more Worcester sauce or a shake or two less Tabasco may result in a snapped 'Well, you do it then.' Only the clatter of dishes prevents the assembled throng from hearing your whispered 'I usually do.'

Post-Jamie Man

He knows his virgin from his extra virgin, his cod's roe from his bottarga and his parmesan from his pecorino. Today's man-in-the-kitchen is informed, enthusiastic and above all confident. He is as happy there as he is in the garage, in fact probably more so. And if he isn't confident, he certainly isn't about to show it. His motto may well be, 'If you can't dazzle them with brilliance, then blind them with balsamic.'

He reads the weekend cookery supplements, has all the latest chef's cookbooks, watches every shouty, full-of-himself chef on television. His hero is probably Gordon Ramsay, mostly because of the *über*-chef-turned-entertainer's background as a footballer. Yet in truth he owes his new role in the kitchen more to Jamie Oliver, who despite being determinedly mainstream himself has helped to make the whole subject of cooking 'OK'. Whereas Gordon has given men the thumbs-up to be seen in charge of the home stove, it is actually Jamie who has made them feel that picking up a wooden spoon is a perfectly normal thing to do. It is fine to spend as long picking a melon as choosing a chisel, to have a favourite rolling pin just as you might have a favourite trowel, to be seen tasting olive oil at the local delicatessen. Just as long as you do it in trainers and not a pinny.

The new-man-in-the-kitchen is obsessed with kit, with ovens like racing cars, Japanese knives that cost as much as a lawnmower, vinegar the price of a bottle of champagne. Post-Jamie man must have the right tool for the job, even if he doesn't quite know how to use it. It is now *The River Café Cookbook* that is by the bedside rather than a guide to fly-fishing. If the young are queuing up to go to catering college, and twenty-first-century man is as happy at the chopping board as in the potting shed, it is to Jamie Oliver we should bow.

If You Can't Stand the Heat

It will probably come as no surprise to learn that there is a website called Danger Men Cooking. Even less so that it is the home of the Serious Sauce and Accessory Company. Sauces are sold in two heats, 'Firemud' and 'Wussy', and you can also buy the sort of wide plastic tape that the emergency services use to cordon off road accidents, but bearing the legend 'Danger – Men Cooking'.

Another site suggests forming an all-male cooking club for puttanesca-and-poker evenings. Presumably it has to be that particular sauce (puttanesca being the only one named after a hooker) and that card game ('poker' has a certain ring to it) so as not to cast a shadow of doubt on the participants' unswerving masculinity. Presumably in case someone accused them of starting a tray-bake circle. Personally, I'd rather have a nice 'penne-and-patience' evening than have my meat seasoned with a (D) cup of testosterone.

Scratchings

Curly, golden brown, not unlike a hobbit's toenails yet so obviously of the pig, scratchings have a following all over the Midlands that could almost be described as fanatical. You find them in large bowls on the counters of traditional butchers' shops, sold by weight, often in small greaseproof paper bags or ready-packed in a grocer's shop or off-licence (known locally as 'the offy').

You dip into them on the drive home as you might into a bag of toffees. Locals will travel miles for a bag of really good scratchings, by which they mean crisp, light and chewy, nicely salted but not to excess. Imagine cold pork crackling crossed with a Cheesy Wotsit and you are almost there. Out-of-towners are wary at first, but shortly after the first one dissolves in their mouth they are to be found asking for another. Having initially turned their nose up at the thought of nibbling crisped-up and salted pig's skin and fat, it is not unknown for them to be hooked within one sitting.

Those who remain perplexed by the interest in these crunchy snacks are generally those whose experience has been confined to the over-salted, additive-ridden bitterness of some of the commercially produced versions. A true scratching is as addictive as a class-A drug, and will probably do you about as much good. I have never fathomed why these delicacies aren't more popular further south. A delectable by-product of the lard-making process (they are the bits left behind after the fat has been rendered), scratchings are truly one of England's treasures.

The perfect pork scratching should:

Be distinctively porcine in taste.
Have a thin layer of crisp, bubbly skin and soft fat.
Possess just the right balance of tooth-jarring crunch and melting softness.
Be made within a couple of miles of Walsall in the West Midlands.

Aficionados regard the presence of the occasional hair on their scratching as a good thing. No, really.

A bag of pork scratchings is on my list of desert island foods.

Chocolate Éclairs

The French have their darling little *petit choux* the size of a large gherkin. We have the submarine-sized éclair. It takes endless huffing and puffing over a hot stove to get the flour, butter and water to take up all the beaten eggs needed to make your long buns rise into elegant éclairs. Worse still is the farce of having to squeeze the resulting sticky dough through the nozzle of a piping bag. And then you find you need a second, dry one in order to fill your buns with cream. I'm not really sure that anyone should actually admit to owning a piping bag, let alone a spare. Better to buy these glorious treats from a baker's, but only one where they fill them with fresh double cream and each one sports a strip of the glossiest chocolate icing on top. The only way to eat a chocolate éclair is straight from its white paper bag on the way home, no matter what your mother told you.

The Sweet Shop

When I had been particularly good – or, as I suspect now, my father had been particularly bad – he would drive me to the sweet shop on Coleway Road. On the wall behind the counter were row upon row of sweetie jars, their lids so round and wide the assistant could barely get her hand around them. There were sweets of vermilion and rose, saffron and lemon, and twists of amber and green. Pear shapes, lozenges and elegant little comfits, wine gums with 'port' and 'brandy' embossed upon them, and black-and-white humbugs as shiny as a Venetian marble floor. Some shone emerald and deepest ruby like precious gems, others pale and delicate in old-lady shades of violet and lavender. Fairy drops and barley sugars, chocolate toffees and midget gems, fruit jellies, glacier fruits and sugared almonds, all imprisoned in glass jars so large it took two hands to upend their contents into the weighing scales.

Dazzled, confused and strangely ambivalent, I would ask for the little chocolate buttons covered with gritty, multicoloured sugar dots called rainbow drops, or perhaps some Parkinson's fruit thins, which were rather like flat glacier fruits but with sharper, more distinct flavours. As much as I delighted in seeing the sweeties in their jars, I never quite had as much of a sweet tooth as my father, with his love of American hard gums, wine gums and chewy Brazil nut toffee.

Nowadays I would probably appreciate them more than I did then, though now it would take more than a five-minute car journey to get my hands on a true Ponte-fract cake or a quarter of dolly mixtures. There were the sweets that old people ate – barley sugars, Parma violets, fruit sweets in tins, Newberry Fruits – and those that no one over twelve would be seen dead with: flying saucers, Anglo bubbly and black jacks. There was a pressure to conform to certain sweetie stereotypes, and I know I bought Everton mints and aniseed balls simply to fit in with the other boys at school, when I really, desperately, wanted to buy jelly babies, sugared almonds and floral gums. In other words, 'girl's stuff'.

Nowhere else in the world have I encountered such a nationwide interest in sweets as in Britain. Nowhere have I encountered a newsagents where you have to lean over a counter full of chocolate bars in order to pay for your daily paper. And where else do you find quite so many different types of boiled sugar confections, about two hundred at the last count?

What is it that so tempts the British, and those in the North especially, to the satin stripes of a humbug, the long strings of a warm caramel, or the mouth-puckering heart of a sherbet lemon? The appeal of sugar is obvious, but why is our need not satiated by a little lump of marshmallow or a tarte aux fraises like the French, a slice of chocolate cake like the Austrians or a wedge of turron like the Spanish? Where on the rest of Europe's shelves are the cream toffees, butterscotch, peppermint creams, barley sugar, Smarties, Milky Ways, buttermint bon bons and brown sugar fudge?

I have long suspected that the sweet is a replacement for the thumb we sucked as a child, which was itself the replacement for our mother's breast. Our soft spot for the sweet may well be due to the sense of calm that ensues as the sugar dissolves in our mouths. Let an old-fashioned sweetie slowly dissolve on your tongue and it is as good as turning the pages of a photograph album.

Save the odd bar of Golden Cup, the confectionery we grew up with is still there, albeit not as easy to find as it was. No longer is there a sweet shop on every corner. Could this apparent demise of the gobstopper, the chocolate toffee and the humbug point to a lessening of the nation's need for the comfort of sugar, or have the endless health warnings finally hit home? We still consume a vast amount of confectionery, but the majority is by the young and the elderly. Pensioners buy approximately twice the amount of sweets that twenty-five-to-thirty-four-year-olds do. In fact, those middle years are when many of us lose, by choice or by perceived necessity, an interest in confectionery. It can't go without comment that this is also the age group with the highest levels of gym membership, and the core audience of 'you are what you eat'-type television programmes. It is an age when we worry about how we look, how much we weigh and the state of our teeth. I would also add that it is the time in most people's lives when they are, one way or another, probably the most sure of themselves, and so are less likely to need the humble reassurance and comfort of sugar. A bad day, however, will often see even the least sweet-toothed diving for a bar of Dairy Milk.

It appears that it is during the most difficult periods of our lives that we buy the most confectionery – the painful teenage years, the uncertainty of old age. We go out of this world as we come into it – no hair, no teeth and, so it would seem, with a taste for sweet things. Or is it simply that those are years when we need the most comforting, the most reassurance for what lies ahead – life, death?

The Berni Inn

As a family, we never went out for dinner unless we were on holiday, but there were occasional Saturday lunches at the local Berni Inn. That is where I got the bug of wanting to wait at table when I left school. There was something distinctly glamorous about the Berni Inn, with its mock Tudor beams, smell of grilled steak and plaice, and whiff of lager-and-lime.

Saturday lunch was a milestone meal, in that I was allowed to choose my own dishes from the menu. I stuck safely to things I had seen my parents with: melon, cut into a boat with an orange sail and a maraschino cherry, followed by steak garni, medium rare. 'That'll be very bloody. Are you sure?' my stepmother would ask, followed by a shudder at the thought of it. My dad, for whom a steak should be so raw its veins were still pumping, would say, 'Leave him be. He knows what he wants.' Steak garni always sounded so much more exotic than plain steak, despite the fact that the 'garni' was actually only half a tomato and bit of cress. Still, it made me feel like the bee's knees. No one else at school had even heard of steak garni.

Lunch

Lunch, which is generally taken around the middle of the day, used to be called dinner, and in some cases still is. Christmas dinner is Christmas dinner no matter what time of day you eat it, and no one has ever heard of a 'lunch lady' looking after school meals. The word itself is an abbreviation of 'luncheon', which has always sounded too grand for its own good. 'Lunch', like 'munch', is more casual, and seems more appropriate for a light meal. Initially it was the meal that was shoe-horned in between the two much more substantial meals of breakfast and dinner (which, to add to the confusion, was often called supper).

For some reason, I suppose because it has a whiff of silliness to it, I prefer the term 'nuncheon', which was the medieval term for a bit of bread and cheese, probably accompanied by ale, that was taken at midday. It was what kept farmers going till tea time. Later, in the 1800s, it would have been normal for a craftsman – it nearly always was a man – to go home for his midday meal, though the habit became less popular over the next century, and was soon superseded by a version of the packed lunch.

Initially, this was a meal of 'finishing off' rather than proper cooking. You might 'finish off' yesterday's roast lamb, or maybe serve the leftover potatoes and greens in the form of bubble and squeak. It was when the pickles came out, and the potato salad, together with cheese and biscuits or fresh fruit. This may explain why the sandwich is so popular, a leftover from the days when leftovers were eaten between two slices of bread rather than left to dry up in the fridge and be thrown out a week later. 'Makes a nice luncheon dish,' say so many old cookery books, especially when talking of rissoles or stuffed marrow, or some other silk purse carefully hewn from a sow's ear.

If you eat lunch in Sweden, you will find the meal more substantial than here. It will almost certainly be hot, and garnished with some form of potatoes. No dessert to speak of, just coffee. There is something that appeals about this form of eating compared to stuffing a sandwich down your neck. There is nothing sophisticated about it. It is just meatballs or a piece of grilled fish and some potatoes, yet somehow it is so much more civilised than a carton of soup eaten at your desk.

Crumpets, Pikelets, Muffins and Their Purpose

The only true essentials of a winter tea are a pot of tea and a plate of crumpets, butter nestling in an almost melted pool on the little pancakes' toasted crusts, the holes, all 50 of them (at the last count) full to the brim. In a perfect world, the butter – in this case I think it should be salted – will run down your fingers as you tear at each freshly toasted crumpet with your teeth. You should never cut a crumpet. You sort of tug and suck at the same time.

I insist that there is a season for crumpets, just as there is for hot cross buns or, for that matter, Christmas cake. There should be an 'r' in the month for a crumpet to be truly welcome on the tea trolley. A cushion of yeasty, punctured dough, pillow-soft and laden with warm butter, can only ever be an autumn or a winter thing, as wrong in summer as a strawberry tea on Boxing Day.

Crumpets are easy enough to make if you have flour, milk, yeast and bicarbonate of soda. You make a thinnish batter, and pour it into little rings – pastry cutters will do – sitting on a flat griddle, though a heavy iron frying pan will work. The surface of each little pancake will be alive with bubbles, which then burst and become the crumpet's characteristic holes. A frugal piece of bakery, yet with anything capable of holding that much melted butter, one assumes it could only have been designed by a lush.

A pikelet is a crumpet that has been made without the constricting action of a baking ring, so it ends up flatter and with thin edges rather than straight sides. If you make them yourself you tend to end up with all manner of funny shapes as the batter ebbs and flows on the griddle. Attempting to make a batch for tea last Sunday, I mused at how many of my somewhat flat attempts resembled a map of Wales – appropriately enough, with the Welsh for pancake being *crempog*, itself only a short jump from 'crumpet'. Their delightfully unpredictable shape makes them unsuited to the restrictions of commercial packaging, a fact that has surely led to their virtual disappearance. Perhaps more pertinent is the fact that, being thinner, they hold considerably less butter than a crumpet, which I suspect is really the clue to their downfall.

A muffin is also baked on a griddle, but it has a spongy, bread-like texture and perfectly flat sides. The top and bottom of the thick, fat bun are singed on the pan and the sides are left pale and soft (soft enough for a thumb to be inserted purely for the purpose of tearing the muffin into two halves). You then toast the torn side of each half and butter it with generosity. As with crumpets, I find it easiest to top each one with a slice of butter and then pop them back in the heat so that it forms a pool. The tearing action is not an affectation. If you cut a muffin with a knife you will end up with something flat and uninteresting, and strangely heavy. Cragginess is a bonus when it comes to toasting things (see page 238). Not to be confused with an American muffin, which despite its popularity is little more than a fairy cake with attitude.

Good though the soft, doughy griddle-breads are, I have always suspected that their sole purpose is to provide an edible sponge for transferring as much melted butter from plate to mouth as possible. A buttered crumpet weighs in at 60g, a round of toast at 52g. I rest my case.

The Death of the Chocolate Cake

Once, chocolate cake was something that you took home after a party, its layer of sponge and buttercream held safely between the folds of a paper serviette. Wise mothers knew to serve the rich slice with its crown of multicoloured Smarties as a takeaway, no doubt in order to prevent it from coming up again during the musical bumps.

In the early 1970s we discovered the Shwarzwälder-torte, but rather than do battle with its sensuous but tongue-defying moniker we decided to translate it as Black Forest gâteau. This took our innocent, homely chocolate cake and dressed it up with whipped cream and chocolate curls, or in its eventual humiliating guise, chocolate vermicelli and glacé cherries. The lovingly whipped and sweetened cream of the original sumptuous recipe all too often came from an aerosol can. To add insult to injury, most examples were eaten barely thawed, the last resort of the secretary desperately looking for something with which to toast an office birthday.

Too bad, but by now we had become rather taken by the idea of the moist chocolate cake enjoyed throughout the rest of Europe. This could have led us towards the exquisitely damp and minimally decorated Sachertorte, a shallow Austrian creation from the eponymous hotel on Vienna's Philharmonikerstrasse. With its thin line of apricot jam and easily shattered chocolate coat it has the perfect balance of sweetness, sharpness, moisture and crispness that has made it a world-class confection.

Instead we took the muddy route, starting in the 1980s with the truffle cake, a dessert that contained a lot of high-quality chocolate and double cream, but little else. In essence, a chocolate truffle without the essential crisp shell that would have rescued it from cloyingness. Add to this, a decade later, the endless poor imitations of the River Café's original, gorgeous and bitter-sweet Nemesis, and no wonder our happy little birthday cake has been reduced to something indistinguishable from a failed chocolate soufflé.

The Corner Shop – Our Little Life-Saver

The urbanite's life-support machine, it is the little shop on the corner to which we turn for milk, bread and the occasional 'thing in a tin'. This is the last resort of the hungry, a place that only really enters the picture when we have nowhere else to go for milk or a lemon, or have run out of eggs in the middle of a recipe.

Treated as the place to buy batteries in an emergency, the urban corner shop truly comes into its own when we are a bit drunk and have an uncontrollable urge for a bacon sandwich or a packet of crumpets. It is then, in those hazy, slightly wobbly moments shortly before the proprietor pulls down his shutters for the night, that this little Aladdin's cave becomes our best mate. Even if the bacon we buy is Danish and wet, and the bread is of the sort we usually wouldn't dream of having in the house, at this moment we love the corner shop, and vow to do more of our shopping there. Look, they have fruit (oranges, a few dying apples and a hand of over-ripe bananas), vegetables (a bag of potatoes, their skins turning green in the fluorescent light) and even yoghurt (each one with half a dozen colourings and as much sugar as a bottle of Coke). From this moment, we vow to do all our shopping there, just to keep them going. And how DO they keep going?

Yet, as dawn breaks the next day, and we survey the scene of crumbs, crusts and open packets on the kitchen counter, we shudder at the sell-by date on the packet of bacon, wince at just how much of the white-sliced loaf we managed to get through in the hour or so before we finally collapsed into bed, then bin the offending remains and their e numbers. As we down our first coffee of the day, we forget about the little shop that saved our life last night. At least until next time.

Carving

You start with long, self-important strokes that produce thin, elegant slices large enough to cover one side of a dinner plate. The knife is murderously sharp, partly because you have spent a good fifteen minutes making it so with that swish-swish sound of knife on steel. At first it all seems so easy. It is only towards the end, when the rest of the family is done, and you have got to your own serving of beef, that it all goes tits-up. You eventually resort to hacking the remaining bits of meat off in lumps, dollops, shreds and crumbs. Even so, you still have everyone's attention and more.

He who carves has control of more than just who gets the parson's nose. He is alpha male (or very occasionally female), and as such has charge of who gets the fat, the lean and the crusty bits. It puts him in a position – in charge of the roast – that at first seems enviable; but then you start to realise all the baggage that goes with the responsibility. With only two crusty ends to a joint of beef, and one wishbone to a chicken, the politics of who gets what can be too much for even the strongest alpha male and his carving knife.

My father seemed a good foot taller when he was carving the Sunday roast. He would stand towering over us at the head of the table, all puffed up like a Beefeater. He would brandish the old bone-handled carving fork and knife with an obvious sense of pride. It must have been the joint of beef he was proud of. It certainly couldn't have been his family.

He always did Auntie Fanny first. If she got hers before anyone else, then there was the faintest possibility that she might not still be soldiering on with her stone-cold meal half an hour after the rest of us had finished.

I was served almost last, because I liked my beef bloody, as did my dad, and so needed to have the meat from the middle of the joint, after my brother's crusty bits, Mum's 'Not too bloody, thank you, dear,' and Dad's burnt bit of fat. There was always plenty left for cold, which used to magically disappear overnight. My guess is that my dad ate it after we were all tucked up in bed, with some of the dreaded pickled walnuts of which he was so fond, and which I decided looked like the things that hang off the back end of a sheep.

Haggis, Tatties and Neeps

The haggis isn't as Scottish as it thinks it is. It is only since the eighteenth century that this oversized faggot has been so firmly linked with the north, due to Robert Burns's 'Address to a Haggis'. The final act that secured the haggis's place in Scottish gastronomy came in 1851, when Edinburgh's literati adopted the already-established practice of honouring the late poet with a bells-and-whistles haggis dinner.

On Burns Night, which normally takes place around the poet's birthday, 25 January, the dish is brought into many a dining room aflame, in some cases attended by pipers in full regalia, though presumably with no knickers. I tend to come over all emotional whenever I hear bagpipes playing – they strike a chord with my tear ducts – but even so, there is so much brouhaha about this recipe that often one cannot help being ever so slightly disappointed.

Some sort of ball of minced entrails wrapped in a sheep's stomach has certainly been around since medieval times, and it has been made with calves' and pigs' innards too. Now it is almost exclusively made from sheep's entrails – by which, gentle reader, I mean boiled lambs' lungs, fat, flanks and oatmeal packed into a sheep's stomach, or as is now the case a synthetic substitute or a length of beef intestine. It is not a recipe for the faint-hearted. It is a dish born out of frugality and the wish to use up every part of the animal. There is no other use for the pluck and stomach of a sheep, at least not in daylight, so whoever had the idea of turning them into such a splendid feast is to be commended. Necessity turned into glorious ceremony.

Uncooked, a haggis resembles an enlarged scrotum. Once surrounded by holly and much toasting it looks marginally more appetising (but then, so would a scrotum), though a few glasses of malt whisky will help you appreciate its mild, offally flavour all the more. Tradition has it that you serve haggis, after it has been cut with much aplomb, with mashed potatoes and swedes (see page 100).

I have met many a Scot who wouldn't touch what has become their national dish, insisting that it is actually just a joke on tourists. Reading the list of ingredients, one cannot but wonder. I have had occasion to think the same about Korean kimchee, Chinese congee and on one occasion Cornish pasties, but that is another matter.

Gilding the Lily

There are, I suppose, occasions when a mere spreading of butter on toast is not enough. Some of us regard the addition of anything more exotic than salted butter as excessive, and by purists it will be viewed as an intrusion. However, at breakfast, marmalade, jam or honey is almost universally accepted, if only to appease the British palate and its insatiable quest for sugar. Still, it is only right that some preserves should be more suitable than others: thick honey, especially heather or other blossom, is both energy-giving and gentle on the tongue. Runny honey is simply an accident waiting to happen. Damson, plum, quince, gooseberry and blackcurrant jams have the necessary sharpness for bleary-eyed consumption. Raspberry and strawberry are surely more suited to afternoon tea, though even then most of us find strawberry jam simply too sweet for anything but scones.

Lemon curd, chocolate spread and peanut butter have their fans, but come perilously close to turning our main candidate for gastronomic excellence into a dessert.

Cake and Cheese

In the north of England it is not unusual to eat cheese with your Eccles cake. Some people find this a little strange, or even disconcerting. The truth of the matter is that it is no different from the Spanish habit of serving sweet quince paste with a slice of manchego cheese, or indeed having a lump of cheddar with a slice of apple pie.

Everton Mints

Legend has it that this rectangular mint with its crisp coat and soft filling is named after the Toffee Lady, a large woman who would, at half time, throw handfuls of mints into the crowd at Everton football matches. The crisp, then tantalisingly chewy, mints were first made by Mother Noblett's Toffee Shop in Everton, Liverpool, and are striped like Everton's original football kit.

Welsh Rarebit

Nothing pleases me more than finding those two words on a restaurant menu. It is proof that the world has not quite lost its senses.

Welsh rarebit is sometimes thought of as just cheese on toast, which is what people call it when they want to patronise it. The point is that a rarebit contains beer and mustard (you allow the grated cheese to melt into the beer in a saucepan), which makes a layer the texture of silk to sit on top of your toast. A rarebit has a piquant bite, a suavity and a pleasing savour that no cheese on toast can ever have. Of course it is more trouble to make, which is why this delicacy – there is no other word – has gone out of favour. Shaking a drop or two of Worcestershire sauce over grated cheese can never have the same effect as the slow stirring of farmhouse cheese, mustard and beer. Perfection is reached when the topping has browned gently under the grill and the edges of the toast are charred here and there.

Junket – The Clue is in the Name

Junk mail, junk shop, and of course the porn slang for semen. (What do you mean you didn't know?) This wibbly wobbly custard lies somewhere between the filling of a custard tart and particularly fresh yoghurt. For this we can at least blame the French. The name is derived from *jonquet*, a little rush mat used to drain fermented cream to make a fresh cheese. Elizabeth I ate it with fresh cream, and it has from time to time been flavoured with both rosewater and cinnamon. It is the most tender of all our desserts, its surface soft like that of a crème caramel, its texture that of a lightly cooked egg. Once disturbed by the intrusion of a spoon it has a tendency to break up. Oh, and it must be served at room temperature. Seconds, anyone?

Tunnock's Teacakes

One of the downsides of a distinctly middle-class childhood, and there were many, was that we got Cadbury's Mini Rolls instead of Tunnock's Teacakes. (We also got lemon barley water instead of Vimto, but that is another matter.) Good as the Mini Roll was, with its delicate chocolate and its swirl of cream, it wasn't half as much fun as a Tunnock's Teacake. Matters were only made worse by the fact that my best friend Warrell always seemed to have one on his tea plate, alongside the two Jammie Dodgers and the three Cadbury's Milk Chocolate Fingers.

It is a delicate operation to unwrap a Tunnock's Teacake without cracking the fine dome of petal-thin chocolate that covers the marshmallow centre. There is always a faint disappointment should you peel off the silver-and-red foil to reveal that the crown has been shattered like the shell of a soft-boiled egg.

From the thick disc of sweet, pleasingly gritty biscuit at its base, to the white, creamy froth at its core, the chocolate teacake has nothing nutritionally in its favour. It is sugar, plain and simple. Yet just seeing the box, and gazing through the plastic at its fragile cargo, takes me back to the lunchboxes of my childhood – or more accurately, to other kids' lunchboxes. It is amazing the amount of currency a schoolboy was expected to part with for a classmate's Tunnock, but I always did. I seem to remember one once cost me a whole packet of Refreshers.

Poaching

That is, as in cooking something gently in water, not nicking rabbits off the landed gentry. Simmering meat and fish in seasoned water (onion, carrot, parsley, peppercorns, lemon) will keep it moist, which is essential if it is to be served cold. Be it salmon, skate, gammon or a silverside of beef, the ancient art of bringing something to tenderness by letting it blip and blop in not-quite-boiling water appeals not because of its robustness, but for its gentle tone. Poached food is restrained, calm and delicate, food that whispers rather than shouts. One of our most famous dishes is poached salmon, which is usually cooked whole and served cold with a cucumber salad and a bowl of mayonnaise, or more correctly (but less likely) salad cream. We will ignore the irritating habit of garnishing the poor thing with tomato roses.

The Cookery Hen

A breed of British cook who lives for the recipe. Every cookbook, every monthly cookery magazine, is bought religiously – they (by no means always female) are named for the way they peck through the pages as if picking up crumbs off the farmyard floor, and they have even started taking recipes off the internet. There is no cookbook they haven't thumbed through, and no recipe for ten-minute sticky chocolate cake they haven't tried. Though of course they are quick to point out that none of them works quite as well as Delia's.

The cookery hen is a recipe junkie, following them to the letter and even discussing them online in internet forums with fellow hens. 'Mine took a good fifty minutes at 190°C/gas 5, on the middle shelf, and the recipe clearly said forty-five. Has anyone else had the same problem?' In fairness to them, they probably make a lovely sultana traybake.

The highlight of their year is attending one of the food shows held in vast hangars like Earls Court or the NEC in Birmingham. As they collect their plastic carrier of leaflets and free samples they are sick with excitement at the thought of seeing their favourite TV chef in the flesh. Sitting at the show's cookery theatre (sponsored by a well-known oven manufacturer) and watching a celebrity chef at work is a moment they will treasure all year.

The Oh-I-Never-Measure-Anything Cook

They rarely measure anything, only consult a cookery book for ideas, never quantities or timings, and see no need for a sugar thermometer or even a proper measuring spoon. These are the cooks who glide around the kitchen with a certain calm, whose cakes always rise and who make everything look like so little trouble. They once did a cookery course, but to be honest they didn't really need it. Cooking comes naturally to them, and rarely does anything that comes from their kitchen taste less than delicious.

No one knows if the Oh-I-never-measure-anything cook is born with a natural skill for the perfect guess, or if she picked it up from her mother (who went to Cordon Bleu). All we know is that every cell in her body has a feeling for cooking; she loves it, and eats and drinks enthusiastically. Her kitchen is always slightly untidy, but warm and welcoming, and the food is perhaps a little bit too calorific (she makes a wonderful tiramisu). There is always, always wine with every meal. And often quite a lot of it afterwards too.

This cook has only to eat a dish in a restaurant and she can go straight home and cook something almost identical. No fuss, no panic, she just gets on with it, and the results always look lovely on her Emma Bridgewater plates.

The measure-free cook can turn out a dinner party or even cater for a wedding without so much as turning a hair, bake cakes for her kids' birthdays, and knows how to spot a ripe melon at forty paces. Organised, unfazed and generous, she is a great friend, a great cook and a fabulous gossip.

How to Dress a Scone

You are faced with a plate of scones, a pat of butter, a dish of jam and a pot of clotted cream. This being Britain, it follows that there must be a right and a wrong order in which to dress your scone.

You can have either butter or cream, never both. At least not when anyone is looking. It is generally accepted that the jam goes on first, followed by a teaspoonful of cream. Others insist it is the other way round. Dare I suggest it really doesn't matter?

At a tea shop or hotel you will inevitably get strawberry jam, though many would say raspberry is better. At home I would go for blackcurrant or damson every time.

Bisto

My aunt's little larder, which she called the pantry, smelled of over-ripe bananas (the only way she would eat them) and Izal shiny loo paper. I have no idea why she kept the loo roll in the pantry, I only know that she did. Her shelves, covered in checkered wipe-clean vinyl, were a testament to British icons. There was Ambrosia creamed rice, Carnation milk, Blue Bird toffees, Saxa salt, Oxo cubes, Garibaldi biscuits, Chocolate Wheat-meals, Lion Brand ground pepper, Robertson's barley water and a packet of Bisto. The pale brown powder was as essential to her cooking as salt and pepper. In fact, she used the word 'Bisto', which she referred to as 'Ah Bisto!' after the advertisements, in lieu of the word 'gravy'. She would never dream of mixing the pan juices with a little wine or marsala instead. Gravy was Bisto and Bisto was gravy, and that was that.

The French got the bistro, we got Bisto. Life's a bitch.

Colman's Mustard

There has been a tin of Colman's mustard in my larder for as long as I can remember. I can't honestly recall the last time I used it, possibly to add bite to a bean-bake thick with molasses and tomato purée. I'm sure it is probably still all right, but the label on the tin is starting to spot in places, like a second-hand book jacket.

Until the softer, less astringent European mustards appeared on the scene, Colman's was the first name you thought of when the M word was mentioned. Certainly my father knew nothing but the famous yellow and red jar. Some find its flavour a little uncouth, yet the searingly hot yellow powder made in Norwich has a striking purity to it, a flavour that is clean and clear, and reminiscent of wasabi, the green Japanese horseradish. Colman's have been making mustard since 1814, and are holding up well against the milder, more subtle imports such as Grey Poupon and Maille, the latter of which can be found in my fridge. Nothing really beats a dab of Norwich's finest on the edge of a plate of roast beef, and its strength is its *raison d'être*. As mustard goes, our iconic brand has little of the nuances and fragrance of the French versions, yet it has legions of fans and loyal customers who wouldn't dream of buying anything else for the Sunday roast. They love it for its heat, its eye-watering straightforwardness, and its brilliant colour, that goes so well with the rose pink of a bit of rare topside and a drizzle of gravy. To others, used to the charm of the cooler French brands, a dab of Colman's mustard is simply a punch on the nose.

A Day at the Market

First, catch your farmers' market. Opening days are erratic, to put it mildly. To be fair, some are open for business every Saturday or Sunday come rain or shine. Others might be open on the third Thursday of every month, or every second Tuesday. Except in Lent, of course, when they will move to a Monday. Then there are those that operate only in the summer months, or close on bank holidays. Heaven only knows what happens in a leap year. It is probably safest to assume that on midsummer's day the stallholders will all be dancing stark naked around the Avebury stone circle.

Having found your nearest market and established its opening days through www.farmersmarkets.net, it will be as well to abandon all notion of taking a shopping list. If it has been too wet to pick the plums, there simply won't be any. If the borlotti beans didn't sprout when they should have, then we must go without. This should be seen not as a hindrance, but as an opportunity. Abandoning our preconceived plan and plumping for what is at its best (ripest, freshest, cheapest) means our diet will be all the more varied. Research into The French Paradox has shown that it is variety rather than red wine that is what makes the French healthier than most of the rest of the world. It just means that shoppers have to learn to think on their feet, adapting their supper to suit what is on sale. It is how the French have shopped for centuries. Those incapable of adapting, or unwilling to adapt, may be well and truly stuffed.

It matters that we patronise the market on a regular basis. If the farmer can get out of the sack at four o'clock in the morning in the pissing rain, then why shouldn't we at least make the effort to turn up? True, fair-weather friends are better than no friends at all to a small producer, but such businesses are often run on a shoestring, and depend on making their money when they have something to sell. If we are not there to buy it just because of a bit of rain, then everyone loses out.

Patience, a willingness to adapt and a positive spirit on bleak days are likely to be well rewarded. At a London market on a cool morning in late May I found sixteen varieties of cheese, including seven goats'; locally made butter, both salted and unsalted; ducks, free-range chickens and their lovingly collected eggs. There were eleven different varieties of salad leaves on one stall alone, including mizuna, landcress and sorrel; there were eight types of mushroom, even oyster and shitake; all the usual vegetables, including greens, and seven named varieties of potato. There were eight breeds of tomato, and even home-grown aubergines and chillies. Sure, it was a little short of soft fruit, but there was deep garnet red rhubarb, and strawberries that were some of the sweetest and most deeply flavoured I have ever eaten.

Don't even get me started on the ice-strewn fish stall and its glistening, ozone-scented cargo.

And did I mention the potted herbs, including sweet cicely and borage, the heritage broad beans with their magenta flowers, and the piles of sourdough bread and chocolate brownies? To shop at a farmers' market is to find things produced with passion and love, whose growers make, bake, plant and reap out of a basic need to survive, not to please shareholders and boards of directors. Bring it on, Tesco.

The British Lunch Out of Doors Then

Boiled ham
Tongue
Iceberg lettuce, salad cream
Cress, beetroot, cucumber
Bread and butter
Lemon barley water, Vimto, Mateus rosé
Strawberries, cream
Neapolitan ice cream

The British Lunch Outdoors Now

Chargrilled squid, fresh chillies, rocket
Buffalo mozzarella, basil, tomatoes
Grilled chicken, olives, lemon, rosemary
Focaccia, thin-crust pizza
Goats' cheeses
Panacotta
Peaches, melon, raspberries
Prosecco, Pinot Grigio

A Litmus Test

Here's the litmus test. It's nine o'clock, and the light is drawing in. Dinner is all finished apart from the dessert. There is a light breeze on your bare skin. Do you drape a shawl over your shoulders, light the lanterns on the table and open another bottle? Or do you pick up the plates, mutter that it is getting too chilly, and go indoors? It is our answer to this question that is probably the clue to the future of the British at table.

The Victoria Sandwich

Put this sponge on a table with a yellowing, bone-handled knife alongside, and you have a picture of Britain as seen by our parents and grandparents. Now it's all blueberry muffins and choc-chip cheesecake, but few cakes so successfully conjure up an England of large, soppy dogs, ticking grandfather clocks and village fêtes as the Victoria. Like the royalty for which it was named, it has rather fallen out of fashion, lost under the weight of orange polenta cake and sunken chocolate cakes.

At its best, when the butter and sugar have been creamed till white and cloud-like, before the beaten eggs and flour are added, rather than chucked in all at once as has become the habit, it has a charming fragility to it, like the elderly aunt who probably made it. Raspberry jam is the traditional filling, but home-made plum, damson or greengage are just as suitable, if not more.

Gibbs After-Dinner Mints

So not the posh chocolate version you pass round with coffee, but little chalk-white cushions of soft, powdery mint that crumble in the mouth. I can't remember the last time I saw one, but they are still made. A lovely little mint with a texture of elderly plaster of Paris, but much nicer.

The After Eight Mint

Mints also come covered in chocolate, either as shards of mint-flavoured sugar embedded in dark chocolate, as in the Mint Crisp or the Matchmaker, or as the thick fondant of the After Eight mint. The After Eight relies on the 'bliss moment' for its continued success: that instant when the paper-thin dark chocolate breaks and a little of the mint filling hangs down, poised in mid-air, waiting patiently for your lips to return for a second nibble.

P.S. It is very bad form to put the empty little brown-black envelopes back in the box. There is nothing more dispiriting than flipping through them, only to find they are all empty. Like riffling through a filing cabinet only to discover that the file you need so urgently is missing.

The Glorious British Chocolate Bar

Those genius men and women who invented the best-known chocolate bars might be surprised by their enduring success. I sometimes wonder if we are more fond of our national chocolate bars than of any other single food item.

The curious thing is that there are so few of them, and what is more, that most of them were invented in the space of just seven years. The Mars bar, Black Magic, Aero, Maltesers, Quality Street, KitKat, Rolo, Crunchie, Cadbury's Wholenut and my beloved Smarties were all invented between 1930 and 1937. As Roald and Felicity Dahl put it in their charming *Roald Dahl's Cookbook*, 'In music, the equivalent would be the golden age, when compositions by Bach, Mozart and Beethoven were given to us.'

The chocolate bar – at least these famous ones – is not really about flavour at all. It is about how the ingredients feel in the mouth as they start to melt. The milk chocolate, fondant and caramel that make up the majority of the Great British Chocolate Bar melt together to form a sweet, fatty, creamy mass that literally coats your teeth, gums and tongue. A teddy bear for the mouth. Though personally I feel it probably goes a lot deeper: more like a teddy bear for the soul.

It is this bland, cloying, soothing phenomenon that

really appeals, rather than any true chocolate flavour. So when someone tells you they are chocoholics, they are generally not. Just someone in desperate need of a hug.

A look at the top ten selling bars of thirty years ago reveals many familiar names from today, such as KitKat, Mars, Dairy Milk, Twix, Bounty, Maltesers and Aero. Though a more modern list would probably have lost the dear, bubbly little Aero and gained the even smoother Galaxy (does this country need soothing, or what?).

Rest in Peace

No matter how they try, the chocolate companies cannot come up with anything to compete with their classic bars (though there are a few assortments that have done rather well). They throw us a new bar every few years, but in general these haven't fared well. Some have been very good indeed, but being measured against the big boys such as Dairy Milk and the Mars bar is a tough act for any new kid. Some of those that have fallen by the wayside are much missed, and I feel they deserve a mention, if only to remind us of what could have been.

Golden Cup – A long, thin bar of caramel-filled milk chocolate. The seductively rounded ends and Christmassy white, red and gold foil are sorely missed by all who love the exquisite sensation that is milk chocolate and soft caramel. Modern versions, such as Cadbury's Caramel, just aren't the same, lacking the all-important ooze of liquid caramel as you bite into the bar.

Lucky Numbers – The confectionery trade's answer to bingo. A sort of toffee version of Cadbury's Roses, each sweet had a number on its foil. Even my stepmother thought they were 'a bit common', which is saying something.

Texan – Chewy nougat, chocolate: how could it go wrong? Well, quite easily, apparently. One of Cadbury's less successful bars, rather like their Aztec, a Mars wannabe that failed in the 1970s.

Summit bar – I have yet to meet anyone else who can remember this little bar of cherry nougat coated in milk chocolate. I am unsure whether it was Cadbury's, Fry's or Mackintosh's (no one will actually admit to it), but it really did exist, if only for a moment. Its short life was around the time we were glued to our screens watching Danny Wilde and Brett Sinclair (Tony Curtis and Roger Moore) driving around Monaco as The Persuaders.

The Supermarket Fish Shame

You get to the fish counter, take a ticket and stand amongst the huddle. There are neon salmon fillets that look tempting, pale ones that, despite their organic label, don't. There are mackerel whose iridescence has faded to a drab grey-blue, their eyes dead and distant, and a dish of crabsticks like seaside rock. There are oval shells the size of a side plate holding beige mussels the size of slippers, and dry winkles the colour of dirty slate.

The front of the counter has stained aluminium edges, caked in limescale and dried fish scales. There are bits of unidentifiable yuk in the corners, and there is the faintest smell of urinal about it. Yet it is this, or no fish supper. Sure, there are the neatly packed salmon fillets and mackerels in their slimy transparent coffins, prawns whose labels boast exotic place-names – Madagascar, India, Zimbabwe – and neat squares of haddock. But you want to feel that your piece of flesh came from a fishing line rather than a production line.

The Greengrocer – A Local Hero

No one else writes quite as a greengrocer does on his windows, with his bold swirls and thick upper-case letters. Curious, too, that you never see them doing it. Greengrocers are a dying breed. Nowhere have I found a newly opened shop, only liquidators and 'for sale' signs. With their cubbyholes of pale Golden 'Delicious' apples, these are shops in their death throes.

Those that have closed already, or that are desperately clinging to life, are quick to blame the supermarkets, but the culprit is just as much their unwillingness to change, to accept that their customers are now likely to want lemongrass, basil, chillies and limes every bit as much as they want a pound of apples. That we are past being offered New Zealand fruit at the height of the British apple season, and that no one really wants tangerines in July. They have refused to extend their hours to fit in with the way we now shop, but only because they were 'at the market at four o'clock' and can't afford to take on extra staff. More likely, they don't trust anyone but themselves with the till.

Only the enlightened or the lucky have survived. The fact that they are second-generation and the shop is on a cheap rent has helped some. Others continue to trade simply because they are good at what they do. They are willing to take a risk with a box of figs or a bunch of organic beets. They have not stood still, but have moved at the same pace as their customers.

The majority of British shoppers buy their vegetables at the supermarket, cleaned, pre-packed and ready to cook. Vegetables for the time-poor. There are no odd sizes or mis-shapes, no outer leaves to throw away, and no soil to rinse off in the sink. In fact it is as if they have never been in the soil. Which, of course, many of them haven't. Hydroponics means no dirt or worms, and regular spraying means no aphids. The organic choices are often more numerous at a supermarket than at a traditional greengrocer, and unlike an organic box delivery, you can choose your own. Neat, perfect and packaged, ready to slice and go. It's all good stuff, prettily wrapped and at a fair price, yet somehow, mysteriously, supermarket vegetables manage to lack heart and soul. Even at their best there is something clinical and almost plastic about them.

A Nation of Old Boilers

An ingredient from outer space has landed on the kitchen table. You know nothing about it other than the fact that it is edible. There is nothing else to eat, and you have no choice but to cook it for your supper.

The Chinese would almost certainly stir-fry it with garlic, ginger and spring onions; the Italians might grill it over charcoal and serve it up with olive oil and basil – that is, if they don't chuck it in with the fettuccine. The French would stew it gently with onions and red wine – unless they were in Paris, where they would cut it into thin slices and arrange it on a very large plate with a drizzle of 'jus'. A Thai cook would shower it with chillies and lemongrass, a Vietnamese might add a few lime leaves, while a Californian would shower it with cilantro (after first checking it had come from the right stall at the farmers' market). I am sure a New Yorker would send out for it, while a Swede might well pickle it with vinegar, onions and dill.

Culinary clichés? Certainly. Knee-jerk generalisations? Definitely. National stereotyping? Surely. Yet in practice, probably not a world away from the truth.

So what would the British do with it? My guess is that we would boil it, just as we have boiled everything from the tenderest beef (and surely there is no crueller end) to a sponge pudding. Just as we boil almost every vegetable from sprouts to onions, even though there are far more interesting ways to cook them, and just as we have put every type of meat, fish and fowl in deep water since someone first invented fire.

It is what we do, boil things; and if we don't, then we roast them till they are ever-so-slightly overdone and serve them with thickened gravy and too many vegetables. Boil, roast and occasionally poach, or if it's fish, we fry. It is what we do.

Hotel Toast

Hotels have a distinct way with toast, producing a rack of lightly browned, tepid bread cut into triangles. Even when eaten within minutes of its arrival at the table it still manages to be pliable, stretchy even. The butter refuses to melt, staying sweet and firm on the surface. Yet somehow, there is something perfectly agreeable about this particular hybrid. Bendy, cold, elastic and invariably too thin, hotel toast is still curiously moreish, and feels somehow 'special'.

Dick and Other Delights

Cabinet pudding, treacle sponge, jam roll, apple hat, Sussex pond, plum duff, roly poly and spotted dick – a roll-call of hot puddings to get any public schoolboy creaming his jeans. An orgy of suet, sugar, jam, butter, eggs and fruit, most of these hot puddings were staples of the Victorian table, though some of their recipes are distinctly older.

This is Billy Bunter food, the stuff of undiluted greed, yet many of these puddings served the purpose of filling us up and bolstering our bodies against inclement weather. Currently all are fashionable again, if only as an occasional escape from low-cal, low-fat, did-I-just-eat-a-pudding?! puddings. In restaurants brave enough to put such good things on the menu, there are more takers at lunch, when the sticky pudding is almost exclusively confined to male customers. In the evenings it is the female diners who apparently give in to the charms of apple hat. One can only assume that the average male worries more about the effect a portion of plum duff is likely to have on his athletics in the bedroom than it will on his afternoon workload.

Many of these nursery puds have their roots in austerity, with several of them containing leftover breadcrumbs, windfall apples and scrapings from the jam pot. But it is the cold, keeping out thereof, that is their true *raison d'être*. (Perhaps that should be *raisin d'être*.) Suet and flour is immensely warming to the body and to the soul. You can feel your body temperature rise several degrees after just one spoonful of treacle pudding. By the time you have cleared your plate of every crumb of syrup sponge and each dribble of its accompanying custard, you are feeling distinctly like a well-lagged boiler.

Apple dumplings, roly poly, figgy pudding, treacle

roll, syrup layer – the best-known British boiled puddings roll off the tongue with the sensuousness of a Lucian Freud painting. For every famous name, such as Sussex pond pudding, with its cascading pool of lemon syrup, there are another two known only to collectors of Victorian cookbooks. *Pace* Mrs Townley's apple pudding, Kentish wells, Bedfordshire clanger, Great Western victory roll and Rotherfield sweet-tooth, the final resting place of the Great British Boiled Pudding is the local cookbook, often compiled by members of the Women's Institute. It is here you will find enough sweet dough to keep you warm for the next decade.

Dead Man's Leg

A short list of puddings to die for (and you will).

Spotted dick – A suet roll encasing a filling of currants, sugar and raisins.

Spotted dog – A roll freckled with dried fruit, as Mary Norwak says in *English Puddings*, 'like a Dalmatian dog'.

Jam roly poly – In theory, a roll of suet pastry wrapped round a layer of jam, but I have yet to see one that didn't look like the aftermath of a car accident. No doubt I am not the first: this pudding was often nicknamed 'dead man's leg'.

Sussex pond pudding – A basin-shaped pud of golden suet pastry with a lemon and sugar filling. So named because the syrup runs out as you slice into the crust, forming a sweet pool around the edge.

Bedfordshire clanger – A suet roll with two ends, one savoury, the other sweet. You start with pork, apple and peas, working your way along to a filling of apples, dates and sultanas. Somewhere in the middle lies a gastronomic danger zone.

Cabinet pudding – A steamed sponge with dried fruits and candied peel, for which you will need a jug of custard.

The Glue Factor

It is an inescapable fact that the Great British Pudding is made of flour and water. In other words, our sweet culinary heritage is based on little more than glue. Sure, our puddings are sweetened with jam, or currants, or treacle, or syrup, or honey, or chocolate, or apples, but at their heart and soul is glue – something that cannot be said for a French crème brulée or an Italian tiramisu, or even a New York cheesecake. When people wax lyrical about our wonderful history of home-made puddings they are really talking about our love of paste. Bland, blond and boiled.

The Gingernut

Crisp, hot and addictive. Biting into the basic, hard-as-a-brick gingernut, I always worry that my teeth are going to snap. This dark biscuit with its ginger warmth and burnt-caramel-and-molasses undertones is undeniably on the hard side of crisp, though I would suggest it is none the worse for it. What it loses in tenderness it makes up for in dunkability. It is also the perfect size to dunk into a mug, which is more than you can say for a digestive. This crunchy, faintly fiery member of the biscuit tin will, if dipped for the right amount of time, soften to the perfect degree without risk of disintegrating.

If you go a wee bit upmarket, you will find ginger biscuits whose texture is softer, though with the same essential network of surface cracks. The more upmarket the biscuits, the wider the cracks, the pinnacle being the Cornish fairing, whose fissures are more like fjords, and whose texture carries with it a slight chewy quality too. I have always fancied the idea of a dark-chocolate-coated ginger biscuit, and pounce on them on the rare occasion when I can find them. They do exist, but containing both bitter chocolate and ginger, they are hardly what you would call mass-market.

Perhaps I am not alone in remembering the cake you could make with gingernuts and whipped cream. Left in the fridge overnight, the biscuits softened and the cream took up some of the ginger notes. I have a vague recollection that I once persuaded my mother to make one in the shape of Dougal, the low-slung dog from *The Magic Roundabout*. I seem to remember her being quite proud of it.

Pear Drops

It is hard to imagine that these gritty boiled sweets, with overtones of nail varnish, were once one of our most popular sweeties. The slightly flattened ones, tasting of the grainy Jargonelle pear (and said nail varnish), in muted tones of pink, green and yellow, are reputedly better than the rounder variety. Heaven only knows who eats them nowadays, but one must be thankful that they still do.

Acid Drops

Mouth-puckering boiled sweets that hide their sugar content by a dazzling hit of sourness. Occasionally, you can still find them in their metal tins, which successfully adds a romantic note to their wincing sourness. It's a love or hate thing, really – you can't be ambivalent about food that is so sour it makes you shut one eye when you eat it.

Aniseed Balls

If ever there was a flavour that has dropped from favour, it is aniseed. My schoolfriend Warrell's signature sweet, which he was never without, was a little rust-brown ball, often hidden, half-sucked, in his hankie and kept for later. The best of them harboured a little seed at the centre. I suspect I am not the only person to have taken one out of my mouth mid-suck just to see if it has changed colour from brown to white yet.

Butterscotch

When I was a kid, my father used to buy Callard & Bowser's butterscotch, little rectangles of hard-as-nails toffee suffused with a toasted, buttery quality. I haven't seen it for years, though I gather the memory of it is still much loved by anyone old enough to qualify for a free bus pass. Which of course will soon be me.

A Drop or Two of Sauce

It is hard not to look like a slob when you are drunk. But that is when most Brits choose to eat in public. Not in the morning on the way to the office, rarely at mid-morning break. No, we choose our least attractive moments, when we are inebriated. The spectacle of someone stuffing a kebab with lettuce falling out of it down his neck after a few pints is seen every night on every street corner throughout the land (usually while his mate is having a waz in the doorway next to him). It is part and parcel of our eating culture. It just happens to look as ugly as a Thai eating a takeaway noodle soup looks worthy of a cameraman's misty lens.

My theory as to why we don't do the 'food with wings' thing with any style is that while the rest of the world nibbles on the move, we feel the need to wolf down an entire meal. No chic little crêpe or deep-fried samosa for us. We have to engage in the full Monty of burger and chips, or kebab and salad, or baked potato and beans in a yellow polystyrene tray. No other street-eating culture would dream of eating a meal of that size on the pavement. Another sign of how we haven't got something quite right. They snack and look good; we just look naff.

And to pour icing over the whole ugly cake, much of what we eat in the street seems to end up on the pavement anyway, in great yawning splatters of orange, fawn and brown. Not only can we not get it down with style, we can't even keep it there.

Midget Gems

Larger than floral gums, softer than wine gums, these delightfully chewy sweets, like transparent dolly mixtures, were designed for little girls, yet are almost entirely sold to older men. They take a bit of chewing, and curiously remind one of one's childhood even if you never ate them.

Winter Teas – The Crumpet Season

The fire will be lit, with logs rather than coal, and there will be a cold, wet wind blowing outside. Pink noses and numb fingers will tingle as they thaw out in front of the glowing embers. If there is no fire, and there probably won't be, then somewhere within a few feet of an Aga or a wood-burning stove will do. With access to neither, I suppose you can always huddle round the toaster.

There will be crumpets, toasted teacakes or some such toasted griddle-bread, a brown-sugar cake such as gingerbread, or an almond-encrusted fruitcake and maybe a slice of Bakewell tart. A chocolate cake would go down well, as might a light ginger cake with white or lemon-flavoured icing. Stollen, the German fruit bread with a snowy dusting of icing sugar, might sit comfortably at Christmas time. It is 'foreign', of course, though no more so than a slice of chocolate log – or, to give it its correct name, bouche de Noël – and anyway, it adds a touch of Hansel-and-Gretel-type magic during the month of December. After Christmas, an orange-and-almond cake would be a very fine addition to the four-o'clock feast, especially if you have soaked it with a syrup made from the new season's Italian fruits and given it the merest whiff of orange blossom.

A Muffin Worry

I find it sad that we have lost the nineteenth-century term 'Muffin Worry'. I rather like the idea of a group of elderly ladies, and possibly the odd and no doubt unmarried gentleman, getting together for tea and crumpets to discuss a particularly delicious piece of local gossip. Having always preferred tea and scandal to tea and sympathy, I fancy this must have been the Edwardian answer to posting something on Popbitch.

How to Open an English Muffin

While a round-bladed knife is used to spread butter on hot toasted tea goods, it should never be used to cut them. Scones, teacakes and English muffins are split by inserting your thumbs, both of them, into one side of the dough, just above or below the horizon. You then prise the soft and tender item carefully into two halves. If you do it tenderly it will almost certainly break evenly, though the teacake may take a little tearing too. Feeling the soft dough between your fingers is all part of the pleasure. The point is to get a rocky surface to toast or spread with butter. Some will argue that the matter of breaking bread is simply a question of etiquette. I fancy that such a method ensures an open, rough and therefore more interesting texture.

A Log Fire Tea – Some Suggestions

Crumpets, muffins or pikelets, toasted and generously buttered.

Gingerbread, Dundee cake, banana bread, treacle tart, parkin, Chelsea buns, Eccles cakes, apple cake, seed cake, coffee cake, Christmas cake and chocolate cake all possess the weight, depth of flavour and richness to make them suitable for eating on a day when there is a fire in the hearth and icicles are hanging from the eaves.

Teas should be rich and sweet. The smoky notes of Lapsang Souchong, the bergamot hint of Earl Grey and common-or-garden teabag tea all go down well when there is a chill in the air.

Cupcakes at the Hummingbird

Along with Treacle in London's East End, the Hummingbird Bakery on Notting Hill's Portobello Road has made the cupcake hip. It's a Saturday afternoon in May, and I have had to push my way through a crush at the door. To look at the Kate Moss wannabes and their designer-grubby boyfriends around me, anyone would think we were queuing for class-A drugs rather than pink fairy cakes sprinkled with multicoloured hundreds and thousands. Once past the general stew of attitude and arrogance, and having watched someone take the last violet-coloured fairy cake that distinctly had my name on it, I am greeted by an array of iced fancies of such innocent charm (lemon and vanilla cupcakes anyone?) that I melt into its arms.

There are cakes decorated with candy hearts and sugar strands, stripes of blue-and-white icing and tiny pink rosebuds. There is a chocolate sponge the size of a cabbage, and carrot cake under a glass dome. There are cakes in shades of lilac and rose, lemon and mint green and all made with proper old-fashioned ingredients. The guy who serves me does that tiresome 'I'm too cool to smile at you' routine, presumably in case I mistakenly get the impression that he is working behind the counter in a cake shop, but if you can forgive the bruised ego and the odd cracked rib you receive getting your purchase out of the door, the Hummingbird is truly cupcake heaven.

High Tea

How I longed for high tea, that now pretty-much extinct meal of something-on-toast, sandwiches and cakes. With a ring of both the upper classes and the farmer about it, sectors of society that seemed so much more interesting than the plain old middle ground our family inhabited, high tea was something most of us read about rather than experienced.

Served at about six o'clock, this was a substantial meal for those whose main eating was done at breakfast and lunch, and who lived in a world that is now consigned to soft-focus paintings on the lids of biscuit tins. There were plates of cold ham or beef, potted chicken, fish pastes, and above all eggs, served either on toast or baked in little china dishes. There would be bread and butter, naturally cut a tad thicker than for afternoon tea, fish cakes, and usually a deep fruitcake. All good solid stuff to keep one going till breakfast.

High tea is now consigned to what the band of young Aussie nannies make for their wards, though Waitrose fish fingers have generally replaced the potted meats and there isn't a fruitcake in sight. It is simply called 'tea' or 'supper', and is a meal of mayhem and exhausted over-excitement, the point of which is to get the children fed and off to bed. It is all to do with ensuring that the kids have enough sleep, and is of course nothing to do with getting both them and the nanny out of the way so Mum and Dad can have dinner and a bottle of wine in peace.

The Packed Lunch

Even in its modern guise of black designer object with space for your iPhone, the lunchbox has a homely quality to it. Which is odd for something which is, by definition, not for home consumption. Kids' lunches apart, the packed lunchbox with its neat cargo of sandwich, chocolate bar and piece of fruit seems like something from a time gone by, like pie-crust postboxes, panniers on pushbikes and Gilbert Scott telephone boxes. There is something of the Famous Five lurking in every lunchbox.

For all the charms of dolcelatte and scarlet trevise, crayfish and wasabi, sun-dried tomato and goat's cheese, one occasionally hankers after a nice bit of boiled ham with a dab of mustard. Modern sandwich fillings always manage to sound tempting, and while they relieve the boredom of the long wait at Carlisle railway station, and provide a talking point in the office at lunchtime (new sandwich fillings at Pret a Manger provide the ultimate water-cooler moment), they can never quite hit the spot the way an old-fashioned home-made sandwich can.

Packed lunches are a dying breed, and the person who packs their own rather than someone else's is rarer still. Those who do are generally people with patience and a sense of order, who possess the willpower to get up fifteen minutes earlier in order to make themselves something to eat for later in the day. It must be hell when the alarm clock goes off. There must also, when slicing your ham-and-tomato on white, come a moment when you think, 'Might as well eat it now.'

There used to be an unwritten law that a Tunnock's Caramel Wafer be included in every packed lunch, although the less law-abiding amongst us might have been known to sneak any old bar into the long, narrow margin between the sandwich and the side of the box. Rectangular bars of sesame, dates, apricot, almonds, spirolina, sunflower seed, pumpkin seed and even carageen moss have replaced the layers of crisp wafer, toffee and thin, milky chocolate that make up a Tunnock's.

If you are doing things properly, the bar should be eaten before the apple, to satisfy the appetite, but many of us find it hard to resist leaving it till last, so that we can continue our afternoon with the thinnest layer of milk chocolate and toffee on our tongue and coating our teeth. I'm not sure it matters exactly when you eat a Food Doctor bar with its inbuilt goodness, nor for that matter do I care. For me, it just isn't a packed lunch without a Tunnock's.

In theory, the piece of fruit is either for cleaning the teeth (nothing like an apple for getting caramel off your molars) or is to be kept for later, when your energy starts to flag. Suddenly remembering, 'Ooh, I've got an apple' is one way to get yourself on the road home. Either way, it is invariably never anything more interesting than an apple or a satsuma. A piece of pineapple wrapped tightly in cling-film is a modern possibility, though no matter how tightly secured it is, you will find a soggy patch on your sandwich. Passionfruit, lychees and Sharon fruit are all good ideas for the more contemporary box.

Bananas, *de rigueur* for some, have the unfortunate habit of bruising, or worse, making everything smell of banana. Few smells permeate quite so strongly as an over-ripe Geest. It is the sweet, nutty smell of ham sandwich I want to waft up when I lift the lid of my lunchbox, not the cloying, sickly hit of ripe fruit. A mango is only allowed when accompanied by an entire packet of wet wipes and a clean T-shirt.

Modern additions to the day out, dental floss, chewing gum, breath fresheners and portable sat-navs are fine, but really don't belong in the lunchbox.

Werther's Originals

What I call silly old bugger's sweets. Werther's Originals are the Victor Meldrew of confectionery, the sort of sweet that grumpy people use to soothe their ruffled feathers. You read the *Daily Mail*, you grumble about the state of the pavements and occasionally write letters of complaint to the BBC. You wear cardigans, slippers and maybe even smoke a pipe. You also suck these creamy, vanilla-flavoured sweets. Of course, I'm being unkind – all ages and tempers warm to the brown-sugar-and-cream flavour of a Werther's Original. Yet the only thing that stops me buying them is the unshakeable image of an old codger dandling his cherubic-faced grandson on his knee whilst unwrapping a toffee. Or maybe it's a leftover from my father's warning never to accept sweets from strange men.

The Polo Mint

It is nothing to do with the flavour, the price or the packaging. It is simply the ridiculous pleasure of poking the tip of your tongue through the hole. Only we could have a national food icon that celebrates not what it is made from, but the hole in the middle of it. Not true, of course – the Swiss have their Emmenthal, but then again, what else have they got to celebrate?

Camp Coffee

Yes, they still make it. My aunt would drink nothing but this curious coffee and chicory essence with its tall, thin bottle and label of a turbaned Sikh serving coffee to a kilted Gordon Highlander. Recently redesigned in an attempt to hush accusations from racial equality groups and to bring the product up to date, the label now shows the Sikh and the Scotsman sitting down having coffee together, which is of course much more like life as we know it. The master–servant image has thankfully gone, to be replaced by something less offensive: a picture of two men in skirts having coffee together under the word 'Camp', which is obviously much more acceptable all round. Well, it is to me.

Camp coffee, a tar-like mixture of sugar, water, coffee and chicory root, is considered by many cooks to give the best flavour of all for coffee cakes and icings, delivering just the correct strength without having to make espresso. Someone, somewhere, must still use it to make coffee, though I have yet to meet them. Tragically, Hector Macdonald, the officer on whom the picture was modelled, shot himself in Paris in 1903 after allegations of homosexuality back in Ceylon, an accusation that no one has ever really got to the bottom of.

Camp coffee has been made in Scotland since 1885. It is said to have originated when the Highlanders needed a drink of coffee that could be easily brewed in the field. In the days before instant coffee this certainly made sense. Its appearance on today's supermarket shelves is probably not so much a sign of a great drink, as of just how hard old habits are to kill off. Either that, or home-made coffee-and-walnut cake is even more popular than one imagines.

Robinson's Barley Water

Was there anything quite so depressing, on being offered a glass of squash by your best friend's mum on a hot summer afternoon, as to find her bringing out a jug of barley water instead? Barley water was what goody-goody kids drank, the ones who did their homework on time and who gave out the pencils in class. They were the ones who always had clean shoes and brushed hair, and never forgot their games kit. Of course it is probably my imagination, but I seem to remember them all wearing glasses too.

Barley water, for those who have managed to avoid it, is a cloudy, sharp lemon or orange drink with a curious back taste you either love or hate. Lemon barley is the only drink on earth that actually manages to be grey in colour. Nowadays it wouldn't get past the marketing men, who would probably want to colour it red, but in the 1960s a jug of Robinson's barley water tinkling with ice cubes was as much a part of summer as Wimbledon, cricket and strawberry teas.

There is something gentle about a glass tumbler of this old-fashioned drink. In Victorian times the sugar, lemon, water and pearl barley that go into making it would sometimes be joined by a shot of calf's-foot jelly, to give it a slightly gloopy texture. To this day there is something vaguely wobbly about it, though I remember it being more so when I was a boy. Aware of its history as an invalid drink, parents felt the presence of a bit of barley was a good thing, and quite often a request for a fizzy drink was turned down, but followed by, 'But you can have a glass of lemon barley if you like.'

Out of a Net and onto the Net

The photographs are striking, each plaice, haddock, sole, wet with freshness, irresistible, its eyes twinkling as the textbooks tell us those of fresh fish should. You scroll down to scallops that appear barely to have left the sea, sardines so silver they could be in a jeweller's window. You try to imagine what 375g of halibut will look like. How many will it feed? Will it be enough for two? You worry that if you're not in when the delivery man calls, your fish may end up sitting at the sorting office next to the radiator, or just that bit too close to someone's mail-order compost worms from Wiggly Wigglers. And what exactly is 400g of skate middles for £11.90?

You double-click and double-check. Your order is confirmed, and you forget about it until a few days later there is a hefty knock at the door. What you get for your half-hour online is a neatly packed, odour-free, yuk-free box of fish. It is as fresh as promised, and fresher than expected. It is only as you unwrap the contents from their leak-proof, heat-sealed bag that you realise just how little fish 375g of halibut actually is.

Marmite

Savoury tar for your toast. As shiny as a lovingly polished army boot, saltier than a mouthful of seawater, stickier than treacle, and somehow the work of the devil, nothing quite polarises opinion like a pot of Marmite. I have never met anyone who felt ambivalent about this exclusively British spread – even its current advertising campaign plays on the fact that you either love it or hate it. It is sometimes used as the foodie's answer to Norman Tebbit's 'cricket test'. Though quite why liking or not liking a staggeringly salty, yeast-derived spread only edible in minute quantities should be a sign of one's patriotism is debatable. I am not sure the test even works, as I love the stuff beyond words, yet I am hardly what you might call an anglophile.

The fat, Friar-Tuck jar with its stiff yellow screw cap is not only instantly recognisable, it is unchangeable. The minute some bright young designer comes along with a major change of clothes, the product could be lost. There is something life-affirming about gripping that chubby little pot. Even the new squeezy pot seems something of an impostor, though no doubt we will get used to it. But the yellow, white and red livery and the tubby jar are probably the best-known of any commercial product in the land, and are recognised worldwide. The Marmite jar is as much a national emblem as the black London taxi, the Routemaster bus and the paintings of Gilbert and George. It is a national emblem, at least for those who have the taste for it.

Marmite becomes all the more precious when there isn't much of it. Too much on your soldiers and they become almost inedible. Never has the 'less is more' tag been more appropriate. It is odd, however, that the Marmite jar is either full or virtually empty. You rarely see it half-full. Curious too that even when the pot is empty, it is never truly empty. If you pick it up and turn it left, right, on its side, and poke around long enough with the end of the knife, you will always, always find just enough for another round of toast. Just.

The Organic Box

It seems like such a good idea, and it is. A recyclable box delivered each week to your door, a selection of fresh, locally grown food in season. In summer there will be runner beans that look as if they were picked half an hour ago, and courgettes whose dark skin shines as if it has been polished. In autumn there will be crimson plums that taste the way they did when you were a kid, and in January tight-skinned clementines complete with their leaves. Each brown paper bag is a surprise, a little piece of Christmas every week of the year.

On the downside are the interminable swedes that make your grey winter heart sink, the dismal fact that you never quite manage to use everything up before the new bag arrives, and the inevitable logjam of wrinkled turnips in the vegetable rack.

The Neat and Tidy Cook

'What's the point of cooking when Marks & Sparks chicken korma is just so good?' Why anyone would want to chop and scrub and peel and plate is beyond the neat and tidy cook. This cook buys everything ready-made, and so only qualifies as a cook by the small technicality of putting food in an oven.

The packet cook has no comprehension of cooking as an act of pleasure, hates the idea of following a recipe, and most of all the fact that food is just so messy. The idea of buying organic vegetables that might need to have the soil scrubbed off their faces is as absurd as the thought of buying a chicken that needs plucking. And why buy a vegetable that needs washing anyway, when you can get them washed, peeled, sliced and ready for the pot?

This section of the British public has no feel for food, for the quiet, peaceful beauty of a pure white aubergine, for the soft rose-coloured fuzz of a peach, or for the floury, crackling crust of a baguette broken on the way home from the shop. Not for them the sizzle of a roast being basted in the oven, the heavy silence of a bowl of noodle broth for a solitary supper, the loud laughter of a meal shared with slightly drunken friends. No crisp snap of a newly cut lettuce stalk, no table scattered with sweet crumbs from a fragile fruit tart, or the patina of a much-loved tabletop scarred from years of good eating. For them it is all about a neat little meal in a neat little tray in a neat little house, with no washing up.

A world of sensual opportunities missed.

The Cool, Modern Shopper Cook

It is this type of shopper cook, the one who knows not only the difference between chubby, chalky arborio and long, thin basmati but, what is more, understands why a risotto isn't going to work if made with the latter, who is probably the cook of the future. As we read more about food, and cook more, the point of buying a whole chicken rather than pieces, or of picking up meat on the bone, of spending Saturdays stocking up at local delis and markets, becomes clear. This breed of cook, the modern, thinking cook is the person who spends money on good ingredients and uses them soundly, and for pleasure, rather than as any sort of status symbol. They appreciate the pleasures of cooking well and eating well, and are as happy with a cheap meal of delicately spiced dhal as with a sumptuous organic roast and its trimmings. The CMS is fussy though not obsessive about what he or she eats. They buy what they buy with intelligence rather than extravagance, and have no time for penny-pinching parsimony. Oh, and they usually have a shopping bag – groovy and capacious – with them, rather than arriving home like a clown with an armful of plastic bags.

This is the shopper who knows that a whole chicken makes more economic sense than buying a ready-butchered bird. They are likely to read their broadsheet newspapers, and to know their Hugh Fearnley-Whittingstall from their Nigel Slater. To them, organic is more than just a label: they know exactly why they are buying it, and wouldn't dream of using a battery egg, a supermarket own-brand or anything whose provenance isn't crystal clear. In short, they have made the connection between what they eat, and their own and others' wellbeing.

The cool, modern shopper is absolutely not a food snob, and is as likely to buy PG Tips as a packet of green Guokuro from a tea specialist. They simply happen to like good things, whether that thing has the street credibility of a Jaffa Cake or is something with more rarefied appeal. They are passionate about kit, and have the best knives and saucepans money can buy, do much of their shopping in catering suppliers rather than off the supermarket shelves, and like their equipment heavy. They have all the most high-profile chefs' cookbooks, but are not averse to making the sort of pudding their mother used to make. They bake too, and with the best organic flour, and probably have their own sourdough starter bubbling away in the fridge.

If ever anyone needed proof that we are headed in the right direction, that good eating may yet become as much part of our national identity as it is of the Italians, the Spanish and the French, then this is the person to look at and take heart from.

'Hands that Do Dishes'

Washing up after a meal is more than an act of closure. Wiping the cottage pie tenderly from each plate with a dishcloth or washing-up brush gives time to reflect on the meal, to remind ourselves who cooked it, and more importantly why, and to gently wind down after the peeling, boiling and plating. Washing up by hand can be a strangely soothing, peaceful time, especially if the water is clean and the bubbles glisten pink and blue and green in the light.

Cleaning a plate or polishing a knife can be seen as being a way of caring for someone. It is as much an act of fostering as ironing someone's pyjamas or replacing the loo roll; a way of saying that you care without the awkwardness of saying it. Me, I would much rather they unloaded the dishwasher, a job I hate almost more than any other.

Things Move On

There was a time when we needed a bowl of hot water and a squeeze of Fairy liquid. Now we need a machine, dishwasher tablets, rinse aid, dishwasher salt, a maintenance contract and something called dishwasher cleaner to clean the thing that is cleaning our plates.

Last week I noticed an advertisement for dishwasher freshener, to stop your dishwasher from smelling like a dishwasher. Next thing your dishwasher will want its own masseur and a week off in January to go skiing.

The Death of the Cheese Board

We are slowly coming round to the idea of offering just one fine cheese, or at the most two, in perfect condition. But old habits, particularly those associated with eating, are hard to shift, and the cheese board – a wooden plank dotted with half a dozen bits of out-of-condition cheese – still pops up more than it should do on British tables.

The cheese board, *de rigueur* at almost every dinner party and family gathering since 1962, was at its most popular in the days when well-made cheese was less easy to find than it is now. In the absence of the glorious artisan offerings we now take for granted, those wishing to impress their friends and family with a display of cheese and biscuits as an alternative to Pears Belle Hélène had no alternative but to rely on what was available in the local shop. Hence the Great British Cheese Board was made up of a wedge of red-waxed Edam (known in our house as Dutch Rubber), a piece of Danish Blue, and individually wrapped triangles of Camembert. It was indeed the piercing sniff of Danish Blue, a cheese I have always loved, that gave your dinner party an air of sophistication.

In the 1970s the more experimental of us might have added a foil-wrapped drum of Boursin, and later even adopted the slightly disturbing pink-and-cream-marbled Red Windsor and its green stablemate Sage Derby. The point being to introduce a splash of festive colour, rather than to add anything in the way of interest to the cheese-lover.

There have been other lactic flirtations over the years. Lymeswold, a mild blue cheese as bland as its name, appeared in 1982, only to disappear in 1992. The idea had been for one of the vast dairy conglomerates to turn our surplus milk into something that we could proudly export – hence the cute, but meaningless, name. Sadly, the powers that concocted this little number, and spent a small fortune on marketing it, seem to have overlooked the fact that it tasted of absolutely nothing.

Ten years ago no cheese board could be brought out in public without its regulation wedge of Cambozola, the German-made blue cheese with a creamy texture and curiously fake-tasting mould. Just as Fry's Chocolate Cream is what a true chocolate-lover will have to choose in a chocolate emergency, a slice of this mild, soft blue cheese is occasionally the refuge of the cheese-lover faced with a cabinet of over-chilled factory cheeses. But it may not be for the famously inoffensive flavour that they buy it. I can't be the only person who finds something strangely pleasing about lifting the paper label from the perfectly white bloom in one piece.

The idea of several pieces of factory-made cheese on a block of wood being a match for the wicker tray of haltingly stinky, sensual cheeses you are offered in France should be discarded with immediate effect. So goodbye to those perfectly round slices of smoked cheese, the wedge of yellow-waxed Gouda and the triangular block of 'mushroom Brie'. You will, I'm sure, be well and truly missed.

Thick Toast

Cut from a bloomer or similarly old-fashioned loaf, this is perhaps the *dernier cri* of the toast world. The optimum thickness is a centimetre at the edges, and the colour should always be on the pale side of gold. It must, absolutely must, be buttered while hot. Crusts must stay, and preferably be slightly charred at the very edges. In heaven, there will also be a pool of half-melted butter in the middle.

Best Friends

Toast is the edible equivalent of The Samaritans. Like Colette with her glass of champagne, it has been known to get me out of the depths of despair. On bad days a buttery, crusty slice is the first thing I turn to.

There have been times in my life when I have virtually lived on toast, never tiring of its warmth and sustenance, its crisp, doughy texture being all I need in terms of comfort, and its cost per bite permitting me to get something inside me at even the most hard-up moments.

To those who find themselves alone, either because they live that way or because they have managed to find a minute's peace and quiet, toast often serves as a replacement for a meal, filling a gap with the least possible fuss and washing up. In drunken moments a round of buttered toast will be your saviour, soaking up the drink like blotting paper and lining your tummy.

I suspect that for most of us there has been a point when toast has briefly been our best friend. Maybe we were broke, or busy, or drunk, or lonely, or in need of its crusty, buttery qualities. For many of us, who understand the real point of toast, it may just continue that way.

Treacle Tart

The Americans hold the title for a love of shallow, sticky tarts, with their world-famous pecan pie and its undulating surface of nuts and maple syrup, and the Pennsylvania-Dutch shoo fly pie with its black heart of currants and molasses. Yet somehow we have managed to upstage everybody with an open pastry case full to the brim with syrup and breadcrumbs.

It has to be said that there is no excuse for a pudding of treacle and bread, and that it should be firmly filed under 'occasional treat'. The cast of butter, sugar, flour, golden syrup and bread ensures that there is not a vestige of hope for this recipe in terms of nutrition. Those irritating harridans on television who persist in telling us how to dress, think and of course eat would no doubt rather die than tuck into a slice of this golden, sugary pie. Which is why they are no fun. Leave them to their mung beans. That way there will be more treacle tart left for us.

Coconut Ice

One of the few sweets that can be made successfully at home, though no one older than eight should be caught doing it. Coconut ice manages to seem sweeter than sugar itself. Maybe that extra shot of *sucre* is due to the addition of coconut – whose presence in even the smallest amount has been known to ruin my breakfast muesli – or maybe it's due to the pink and white stripes, which are capable of making anything seem sweeter than it really is. The principle works with people too.

The Cream Cracker

Eternally linked with *A Cream Cracker Under the Settee*, Alan Bennett's celebrated monologue for the late actress Thora Hird, this light, crisp biscuit is as British as anything could ever be. Other countries have them too, though in my experience they never taste quite the same as our beloved Jacob's. The details are simple and quietly perfect: crisp, but not exactly hard, and wrapped in bright orange livery with a black diamond-shaped label holding their proud name. When they are crisp, which it must be said they are not for long, cream crackers beg for a bit of butter and some cheese, though strangely, not the best sort of cheese. Perhaps not wanting to get above its station or to get into fisticuffs with the oatcake, the cream cracker seems improved only by a slightly inferior, corner-shop-style cheddar, a cheese without the benefit of a farmhouse upbringing.

Jacob's cream crackers first appeared here in 1885. It was no doubt their very plainness that appealed to the Victorians, who seem to have regarded anything deeply flavoured as the work of the devil. If blancmange was a favourite Victorian pudding, and a light consommé a popular starter, then it stands to reason that the cream cracker was a favourite biscuit. Demure, delicate, unchallenging, the cracker fitted Victorian tastes like a glove. It is hard to think of anything more suited to English tastebuds. Pale, crisp and cheap, the Jacob's cream cracker goes with pretty much anything. It is also used as an entertainment, with drunken revellers encouraged to see how many crackers they can eat without taking a drink to wash them down. How British can you get?

The truth is that while this thin, square biscuit is thought of as British, it actually originated in the United States, the idea being taken up by William Jacob, who produced the first of his eponymous crackers in Dublin. As if to remind us that they were never really ours anyway, until recently Jacob's was owned by Danone, the French food conglomerate.

Barley Sugars

As a child, you wanted to cry when you asked for a sweet and were offered a barley sugar. Usually associated with interminable car journeys and the aged aunts who always kept a few in their handbag. Often found with a bit of fluff attached.

Nut Toffee

Every now and again, my father would bring home a thin tin tray of shiny toffee with Brazil nuts embedded in it. This was the treat of all treats for him, and he would sit with the tin on the arm of his chair, watching Emma Peel and Steed in *The Avengers*, cracking away at his precious slab of toffee.

Delectable as this confection was, its flavour came nowhere compared to the fascination of the little metal hammer stuck to its surface, the only way you could gain entry to the brittle, nut-encrusted 'taffy', as he sometimes called it. Once empty, the shallow tin trays often found their way into the garden, scattered with bits of bacon rind and Christmas cake as gifts for the birds. I would lie in bed on winter mornings listening to the tap-tap of beak on tin as the tits and sparrows pecked up the crumbs we had put out for them.

Other legendary chews are mint toffees, almond toffees, original cream toffees and, possibly my favourite of all time, the tragically extinct Blue Bird milk chocolate toffee, an admission which probably makes me sound a bit of a sybarite. Quite where the Rolo stands in all this is difficult to say, caramel of course being another world.

If chocolate-lovers' taste is measured by the level of cocoa solids, then toffee-chewers are divided by the texture of their sweets. For toffee-lovers it is all in the chew. From the softly melting Butter Perfection to the hard-as-they-come Toffee Nuts with their hazelnut shape and milk chocolate coating, one's favourite seems to be more a question of tooth pressure than of flavour. Taking the Blue Bird as the childhood toffee, through adolescent infatuation with Toffos and then on to the easily dissolving Butter Perfection, one can't help but wonder if there are seven ages of toffee, rather like the seven ages of man. Though I rather suspect dentures might have something to do with it.

Brown Sauce

Somehow, I knew there was something more than just affection missing from my childhood. The whole family of brown sauces – HP, Daddies and the like – was excluded from our house, but I never thought to ask why. My father loved pickles, even the rubber-ball eggs and the distinctly queasy-looking piccalilli. He liked mushroom ketchup too, and anchovy sauce, yet for some reason he never allowed brown sauce of any kind over the threshold. It has always held a certain intrigue for me, no doubt because of that forced exclusion.

They are all vinegar-based sauces, not dissimilar to American barbecue sauces, and some people like them with steak, chops and egg and chips. Perhaps the mother of them all is HP, made from malt vinegar, spices and fruit, which like tomato ketchup and mustard is something to put on the side of your plate and dip each forkful of food into on its way to your mouth.

Depending on who you ask, HP was invented in 1896 by either Nottingham grocer Frederick Gibson Garton, who christened it HP after the Houses of Parliament or by avid gambler Harry Palmer who, it is rumoured, sold his recipe to Frederick Gibson to clear his debts. Either way, this legendary accompaniment with its famous label depicting the Palace of Westminster became unofficially known as 'Wilson's gravy' in the 1960s after the then prime minister's fondness for it. Apparently he smothered everything in it. Long considered one of the great British commercial products, HP is no longer made at its Aston, Birmingham factory, but has been moved by its new owners, Heinz, to the Netherlands, a move heavily criticised by those who feel it is akin to making Harrogate Toffee in The Hague.

On 2 July 2007, the day marked for demolition, wreaths were laid outside the factory in Aston. One should remember not just those losing their jobs, but the fact that this factory once boasted a vinegar pipeline that took the essential ingredient across the A38. One couldn't help but wonder if it was just a bottle of sauce for which they were mourning, a closed factory and its loyal workforce, or possibly something altogether more intangible.

A source of great pleasure in writing this book has been discovering the many websites set up by both enthusiastic food-lovers and what one could politely call 'anoraks'. Few are more fascinating than those devoted to the whole family of brown sauces. At the time of writing this particularly British sauce seems to be involved in a particularly British bit of controversy. There are growing whispers from habitual HP users that suggest there might have been a little, er, tinkering done to their esteemed and adored product. One correspondent even suggested there had been a certain 'revising' of the original product. None of which can be true, of course. Surely no one would be high-handed enough to mess with something as distinctive as a British Culinary Icon not to mention the risk of offending the fervour and passion that lies behind a much-trusted brand name.

Eating with the Wasps

It is a scene of aching Englishness. The table set out in the shade of a tree; the white cloth with its scalloped edges and occasional embroidered sprig of flowers; the cake stand complete with sugar-dusted Victoria sandwich, the platter of diminutive triangular sandwiches, not to mention the jug of barley water for the children. Afternoon teas in the garden always resemble a scene from a white-linen movie, and can be seen as our attempt at creating a scene of Arcadian living, a show to equal the cliché that is the long trestle table of the endless Provençal Sunday lunch, with its pottery jugs of olive twigs and bowls of *soupe au pistou*. Instead of suitably rustic fougasse loaves and dishes of herb-encrusted black olives, there will be dainty scones, dishes of greengage or plum jam, bowls of strawberries and silver sugar tongs.

Most of all there will be sandwiches: cucumber, tinned salmon, crab, tongue or thinly sliced ham, and maybe lettuce, radish and watercress. Sardines belong on a bridge roll. There will be thin sandwiches on spot-less white bread which will, on pain of death, have their crusts removed. There is no more chance of crusts on an English cucumber sandwich than there is of margar-ine in a Parisian croissant. The tea itself will be lighter and paler than in winter, of a more delicate blend, maybe even herbal or modish green. The cakes will be shallower and less dense than in winter, their crumbs soft and pale rather than dark and sticky with treacle or fruit. And tea will be a longer affair, perhaps interrupted by a game of something, though not anything particularly energetic. A bit of Frisbee or half-hearted rounders is about as much as most of us will manage on a still June afternoon.

Almond, pistachio, a sponge filled with slices of peach or raspberries crushed so that their blood-red juices run into the cream, a meringue perhaps, the cake offerings will be as pretty and as extravagant as possible. Soft fruit is often used to great effect, especially the red and white currants hanging like edible baubles from a butter sponge-cake dusted with icing sugar. Fairy cakes, now more usually known by the more butch American term cupcake, often with pastel icing the colour of sugared almonds, are suddenly fashionable again. The most charming must be the lavender-flavoured ones invented for the Lavender Trust cancer charity by the queen of the cupcake, Nigella Lawson. My own choice for a garden tea would be a few butterfly cakes too, if only for the visual joke.

A Summer Tea – A Few Polite Suggestions

Plain scones with raspberry, plum or greengage jam and clotted cream. Bread and butter and a pot of lemon curd.

Angel cake, Battenberg, cream horns, Victoria sandwich (raspberry jam please, not strawberry), carrot cake, lemon drizzle cake, pistachio cake, almond cake, anything pink, anything that involves soft fruit and whipped cream, financiers, éclairs (despite the melting chocolate), butterfly cakes, macaroons.

Bowls of strawberries, raspberries or cherries.

To drink: lemon barley water, vervaine, limeflower or camomile tea, mint tea, rose pouchong, jasmine, jade oolong, green tea, iced tea.

Britain at its gentlest. The equivalent of the long French lunch, the Italian dinner where you move from restaurant to restaurant for each course, the American barbecue, the Indian wedding banquet and the Scandinavian smorgasbord. The meal we hold up as our national culinary trademark.

Seaside Rock

I'm in Sorrento and the lemon blossom is out, clean and white against the glossy green leaves and a sky the clear, soft blue of butterfly wings. The pavements are thronged with slow-moving holiday-makers, many of a certain age, clutching their bottles of Limoncello, the local lemon liqueur, all looking for somewhere for a nice sit-down. Yes, the silver pound is here, with probably no fewer coach parties than, say, Eastbourne or Margate. There are children and teenagers too, none of whom appear especially bored or out of place. They manage to successfully accommodate all-comers here, save possibly the hairiest of leather-clad bikers on a day trip.

Our own coastline runs for some five thousand miles. It takes in rocky shores and shingle, salt flats, shell and chalk shores. There are piers and lighthouses, promenades and sand dunes, and secret hidden coves. There is also a wealth of good beaches, with clean sand and safe water, and many of these have become our most popular seaside holiday destinations.

It is considered quaint to go to Paignton or Torquay, Bridlington or Filey for your summer holidays now, even with the new interest in curbing our air travel. Some of these towns may have reached rock bottom, but others survive well enough in a slightly shabby, down-at-heel sort of way. Cornwall is one of the few places that are regarded as fashionable, brought about mostly by a renewed popularity of surfing and a thriving restaurant scene.

Spend a day by the British seaside and you will see how very different it is from anywhere else in the world. We have coloured buckets and spades, a refreshing breeze, and probably because of that, bright-coloured windmills on sticks. There are long promenades full of skateboarders dodging the elderly and wobbly toddlers negotiating a walk with their first oversized cornet, and everywhere the smell of seafood. Extraordinary seafood it is too, presented without pretension, or indeed any attempt at style, but instantly recognisable as part of the great British seaside.

Cockles and winkles to eat from paper cups, dressed crab and potted shrimps, jellied eels for the brave. There are plates of freshly caught haddock in light batter with chips and peas, plaice with bread and butter for those who care to sit down, scampi for those happy to eat as they walk. Though one tends to stroll, rather than walk, in such places. Seafood and ice cream are the main culinary draws, and their scent lingers on the air. It is almost impossible not to be hungry at the British seaside – there is little that whets the appetite like cawing seagulls and a sea breeze.

If you avoid a bank holiday (and you really should) and the scorching, charabanc-filled days of high summer, seaside towns have much to offer, especially if you are content with a fish-and-chip tea rather than *quenelles de broche, sauce nantua*. Much as I love all manner of piscine suppers, the highlight of a childhood trip to the seaside was not, for me, the shellfish, but a stick of rock. Pink and white with red letters, or with brown and black stripes like a humbug, or my favourite white with multicoloured stripes, the stuff that tastes like toothpaste. Better still was the stick of rock you brought home and left in the fruit bowl, only for it to be found months later, softened to the consistency of minty, chewable fudge.

Rock is peculiarly of these islands, and indeed, peculiar to only the most mass-market of seaside resorts. It is one of the few types of confectionery that has made no attempt to climb upmarket. But then, how could it? Rock is pure sucrose, glucose and colouring right through to its teeth-shattering heart. It doesn't do organic or free-range or additive-free. Most people don't realise it comes in different flavours, but rock-fanciers, a small, dedicated band of people with, presumably, no teeth, know their strawberry from their pineapple. The most common flavouring is mint, though I remember banana too. Black rock is often a mixture of liquorice and mint, and has a very loyal following.

But for me, rock will always be about colour rather than flavour. Not for this boy the plain pink one with the fuzzy black-and-white photograph of Blackpool pier beneath its brittle cellophane. For me a stick of rock must come in the most colourful maypole stripes of white, red, yellow, green and orange. And I like mine minty, rather than the more adult cinnamon or aniseed flavour.

Whether you suck or crunch, your dentist will love you either way. Crunch and you send shards of sugar into every crevice of your mouth; suck and you coat your enamel with a thin layer of pure, teeth-rotting sucrose. And you wonder why your dentist drives a Mercedes.

Visiting Blackpool, say, it is difficult not to buy into the saucy postcard image of the British seaside. Surely such resorts were invented for naughtiness of one sort or another. One cannot help but wonder at the intentions of Ben Bullock, the Dewsbury confectioner who first invented the long sticks of pink, peppermint-flavoured sugar. It was he who, at the height of all the Victorian prudery, was responsible for sending fleets of demure ladies sauntering along the promenade innocently sucking on sticks of pink rock.

We do the seaside well. It may be tacky, slightly faded and with its sugared-almond paint peeling, but most of us probably wouldn't want it any other way. Those saucy, politically incorrect postcards, hordes of red shoulders and white legs, amber-and-white seafood from a Styrofoam cup and kiss-me-quick hats that blow along the prom in the never-ceasing wind combine to make a very special place. No lemon blossom here, just the sharp, haunting whiff of fresh, vinegary seafood and sweet, stripy peppermint rock.

A National Hero

I sometimes wonder if the sausage has replaced the side of beef as the single piece of food the British hold most dear. There is something cheerful, even a bit jolly, about the sight of a hot and glistening pork sausage on the end of your fork.

No piece of edible craftsmanship, not even the loaf of bread, quite runs the gamut of quality like the banger (so called because of its propensity to pop enthusiastically in the hot pan). Most sausages sit somewhere along a line that runs from delectable to disgusting. At one end – for our own sakes let's start at the top – is the proper butcher's sausage, the sort of portly porkers you will find in local family butchers' shops from Lewis to Liskeard. It has a firm skin that, with patience and just a little tending from the cook, becomes taut and shiny in the pan, skin that takes on a tantalising stickiness and is probably what we like most about this particular piece of meat.

As your fork and knife make their way in, minute fountains of hot juice spurt out, and once entry is finally gained (a decent porker should never be a pushover) the meat inside – a good 20 per cent of which should be fat – will be moist, gently herbal and generously seasoned. The texture is coarse, almost rough, the smell is appetising, and what you have on your plate is an object of complete and utter joy.

Then there is the other end of the sausage spectrum, the mean, uncharitable end. The sausage unworthy of its name will be palest pink, the colour of luncheon meat, the size of your index finger, and will smell of almost nothing, though there may be an unpleasant sweetness if it isn't absolutely fresh. This interloper will have no skin, rendering it pretty much pointless in my book, and is likely to have a texture as smooth as pâté. This is a bad sausage, a weak sausage, a pathetic excuse for a sausage. The similarity to certain cheaper brands of catfood seems to go unnoticed by the millions who buy these in preference to something from their local butcher. Six of these nasty little pinkies cost and weigh about the same as two plump good-for-you ones. The two beauties will both satisfy and pleasure your tongue, the six 'excuse-for-a sausage' sausages will be eaten in a flash and will bring with them no sense of wellbeing at all. Fodder rather than food, and a clear case of bad housekeeping, if you ask me. You could probably travel the world and not find a sausage as bad as the worst of ours. Shame on those who have debased this country's proud heritage of porkery and driven it to such depths.

But when a banger is good it is a glorious, proud and generous thing. A piece of work that will stand up to anything the rest of the world has to offer. I'll take a fine butcher's sausage over the effete little lamb noisette, the beef fillet, the escalope of veal, any day.

You can judge a butcher by the sausage he makes. Though even the best seem to have taken to getting more fancy than is perhaps wise. We grow fine potatoes here too, so perhaps bangers and cloudlike mash, probably with a Hodgkinesque swoosh of yellow mustard on the side of the plate, should really be our national dish. To some the suggestion will be pure heresy, but I like the fact that all comers can afford a good sausage (once they have tracked one down, that is), which is more than you can say for a hunk of prime Aberdeen Angus; and I like its cheekiness too, and its glossy, stick-to-your-lips skin.

All of which reminds me to put in a word for the sausage sandwich, a work of art if the bread is soft and doughy enough, the mustard stinging and the banger so hot you have to move it quickly round your mouth with your tongue before you finally pluck up the courage to swallow.

Sarson's Vinegar

A freezing night in January, and we are driving home after seeing *The Sound of Music* for the umpteenth time. I'm singing 'High on a hill was a lonely goatherd ... layee, yodel, layee, yodel lay hee ho,' unsure if my father has noticed that I'm actually singing 'High on a hill was a lonely goat turd' instead. We have the car windows wide open, even though frost is settling on the pavements and the lights of the city are twinkling in the way they only do when the weather is seriously cold. My father doesn't want the smell of fish and chips (or chish and fips, as he insists on calling it) to permeate the leather seats of his ancient, tank-sized Rover, so we freeze. 'It's not the smell of the fish,' he insists when I plead that I can actually see my breath in the back of the car, 'it's the pong of the vinegar.'

The pong of the vinegar is, to this day, something of a national institution. When it comes to our legendary takeaway, and the food on which the rest of the world seems to think we live, there is only one acceptable vinegar: mouth-puckeringly, eye-wateringly sharp Sarson's. It is arguably the Cillit Bang of vinegars, as far from delicate vinaigre du vin as a sparkler is from semtex, and is our answer to the stinging condiments that accompany the world's most celebrated takeaways: the wasabi of Japan's sushi, the chilli sauce of the Vietnamese spring roll, the yellow mustard of New York's hot dog, and as such it is revered.

It is a matter of taste whether such a powerful condiment successfully makes the leap from the chippy's counter to our own kitchens. For this Sarson's-lover, its acidic bite is at its most welcome when in the presence of hot, thick chips, a wrapping of paper fluttering in the breeze and sparkling neon lights. It is the smell that wafts past you on the pavement when you are at your most vulnerable, that on a cold night in town can set you salivating like no other. Like it or not, it is this, rather than freshly cut lawn, that is the smell of Britain.

The Pink Wafer

I'm eleven, and gently shaking the biscuit tin from side to side to see if anyone has filled it up. I prise off the lid – the top left corner is always a sticker – and the smell of sweet crumbs, and the ghostly echo of biscuits past, waft gently up.

It is difficult to describe the wave of disappointment as I find the only inhabitants of the Peek Freans Christmas biscuit tin are two pink wafers and the bottom half of a Custard Cream. Crumbs have stuck to the cream layer, and the edges are bashed and dog-eared, which makes it a no-go area unless I am completely and utterly desperate. On the other hand, there are the pink wafers.

The pink wafer is the Tim Henman of the biscuit tin; a bit too clean-cut and goody-goody, and though you try to like it, it somehow always disappoints. Despite looking a distinct possibility at the beginning when it is fresh from the packet, it never quite delivers, and ends up looking rather dejected at the end.

Somebody, somewhere, must like the pink wafer, but I have yet to meet them. While you can picture a Jammie Dodger or a Morning Coffee person, you can't really imagine who is likely to take a pale pink wafer by choice. My guess is that it is probably the sort of person who makes their own clothes. It's the white cream layer that bugs me, so thin as to be almost invisible, yet so very noticeable in the mouth. And what sort of biscuit is it that has to stick itself to your lips in a desperate attempt to be liked?